# CHRIS LAFFERTY AND RYAN MCNEIL

# Prime Property

*Extend, Convert, renovate – A Homeowner's Guide to Strategic Home Improvements*

*First published by Chris C Penman 2024*

*Copyright © 2024 by Chris Lafferty and Ryan McNeil*

*©2024 Chris Lafferty and Ryan McNeil. All rights reserved.*

*No part of this publication may be reproduced, stored in a retrieval system, or transmitted in any form or by any means, electronic, mechanical, photocopying, recording, or otherwise, without prior written permission of the authors.*

*Published by Chris C Penman.*

*The advice and strategies contained herein may not be suitable for every situation. This work is sold with the understanding that the authors and publisher are not engaged in rendering legal, financial, or other professional services. If professional assistance is required, the services of a competent professional should be sought.*

*Neither the authors nor Prime Joinery and Construction shall be liable for damages arising herefrom. The fact that an individual, organisation, or website is referred to in this work as a citation and/or a potential source of further information does not mean that the authors or the publisher endorses the information the individual, organisation, or website may provide or recommendations they may make. Further, readers should be aware that internet websites listed in this work may have changed or disappeared between when this work was written and when it is read.*

*The authors and publisher shall have neither liability nor responsibility to any person or entity with respect to any loss or damages arising from the information contained in this book.*

*First edition*

*This book was professionally typeset on Reedsy.*
*Find out more at reedsy.com*

# Contents

| | |
|---|---:|
| *IMPORTANT READ THIS FIRST* | v |
| *INTRODUCTION* | x |
| 1  UNLOCKING YOUR HOME'S POTENTIAL: WHY START NOW? | 1 |
| The Value of Timely Renovations | 1 |
| Assessing Your Needs and Goals | 5 |
| Understanding the Basics of Home Alterations | 8 |
| Types of Alterations | 8 |
| 2  LOFT CONVERSIONS: MAXIMIZING SPACE CREATIVELY | 14 |
| Planning Your Loft Conversion | 14 |
| The Construction Process | 18 |
| Finishing Touches | 21 |
| 3  EXPANDING OUTWARDS: SINGLE STOREY EXTENSIONS | 28 |
| Designing for Harmony and Function | 28 |
| Practical Construction Insights | 32 |
| Interior and Exterior Finishing | 35 |
| 4  GOING BIGGER: TWO STOREY EXTENSIONS | 42 |
| The Double Advantage | 42 |
| Technical Execution | 46 |
| Living with Construction | 50 |
| 5  TRANSFORMING UNUSED SPACES: GARAGE CONVERSIONS | 56 |

| | |
|---|---|
| Feasibility and Planning | 56 |
| The Conversion Process | 60 |
| Making It Your Own | 64 |
| 6  REVITALISING YOUR HOME: INTERNAL ALTERATIONS AND RENOVATIONS | 70 |
| Rethinking Internal Layouts | 70 |
| Modernising Utilities | 73 |
| Decor and Aesthetics | 77 |
| 7  CHOOSING THE RIGHT CONTRACTOR | 84 |
| The Importance of Expertise | 84 |
| Communication and Contracts | 87 |
| Monitoring Progress | 91 |
| 8  BUDGETING FOR YOUR PROJECT | 96 |
| Cost Estimation Basics | 96 |
| Financing Options | 100 |
| Keeping on Track | 103 |
| 9  MANAGING THE BUILD | 109 |
| Scheduling and Timelines | 109 |
| Site Safety and Security | 113 |
| Quality Control | 117 |
| 10  ENJOYING YOUR TRANSFORMED HOME | 122 |
| Post-Construction Care | 122 |
| Evaluating the Impact on Property Value | 126 |
| Living and Thriving in Your New Space | 129 |
| *EMBARK ON YOUR TRANSFORMATION JOURNEY* | 136 |

# IMPORTANT READ THIS FIRST

Hi, We are Chris Lafferty and Ryan McNeil, and We're grateful you took the opportunity to get this book. This isn't just another homeowner's manual; it's a blueprint to transform your property dreams into reality. With over 25 years in general contracting services, house building, and joinery, We've seen firsthand the gaps and misinformation that plague our industry. This much-publicised book is our way of setting the record straight and guiding you through making strategic, value-boosting improvements to your home.

After all, maybe you've found yourself frustrated, trying to secure a fair deal in a volatile market where prices seem to spiral without warning. It's daunting when every quote differs wildly and you're left questioning whether you're overpaying, or even worse, underinvesting in quality. This uncertainty can overshadow the excitement of enhancing your home, turning what should be a thrilling endeavour into a source of stress.

Maybe you've also experienced the challenge of finding a trustworthy contractor. You've likely heard horror stories or perhaps even lived through one yourself, where the work done was subpar, delayed, or drastically over budget. It's a common narrative in the world of home improvements, one that can deter even the most determined homeowner.

Or maybe you've even felt the temptation to settle for less than what you envisioned, simply because navigating through quotes, contractors, and design options feels like an insurmountable task. This compromise can lead to dissatisfaction, with you living in a space that doesn't truly feel like home.

And look, We get it, it's not fair.

The truth is, you're not alone. It seems most homeowners are becoming victims of this erratic market, where clarity is scarce and trust is even harder to come by. This shared struggle is more common than you might think, pulling many into a cycle of hesitation and regret.

That feeling of helplessness, confusion, and even betrayal is palpable. You're supposed to be creating the home of your dreams, but instead, you're navigating a minefield of potential missteps and misinformation. It's an emotional rollercoaster that no one should have to ride alone.

Here's what most don't realise: the real issue often lies not just in finding a contractor but in the absence of a clear, well-informed strategy that aligns with your specific home improvement goals. Without this, even the best contractors can only do so much to bring your vision to life.

And now with the possibility of economic fluctuations, the stakes are even higher. Making informed decisions has never been more crucial as it directly impacts the financial and emotional return on your investment.

It seems most are left in a state of perpetual worry, wondering if they'll ever make the right choices or if their investment will eventually pay off. The fear of making costly mistakes can be paralyzing, keeping you from advancing toward your dream home.

## The Homeowner's Hamster Wheel

As a homeowner, you may often find yourself caught in a frustrating cycle when attempting to improve your home. This cycle, which we'll call the "Homeowner's Hamster Wheel," encapsulates the perpetual loop of pain that many experience when trying to achieve the best value for their money in a rapidly shifting market. Let's walk you through each step in this cycle, so you can identify the pitfalls and learn how to avoid them.

## Initial Excitement

Maybe your journey begins with the spark of inspiration. You envision a beautifully renovated kitchen or a spacious new extension. This excitement is palpable as you start imagining your dream home coming to life. However, this initial thrill soon meets reality.

## Market Shock

As you delve into the market, the costs and options overwhelm you. Prices fluctuate wildly, and the sheer number of choices in materials and styles leaves you baffled. Perhaps you find a quote that seems too good to be true, only to discover later hidden costs or subpar materials.

## Contractor Roulette

Next, you enter the phase of selecting a contractor. Finding someone reliable who can deliver quality work within your budget and timeline feels like a gamble. Maybe you've heard horror stories of unfinished jobs or escalating costs halfway through the project. This step often leaves you anxious and doubting your choices.

## Project Pitfalls

Suppose you overcome these hurdles and the work begins. Soon, unexpected issues arise. Perhaps the work is slower than anticipated, or the results aren't aligning with your vision. Communication breakdowns and mounting frustrations make you question whether your project will ever finish the way you imagined.

## Illusory Completion

Finally, the work concludes, or so it seems. For a brief moment, relief washes over you. However, as you start living in your newly transformed space, small imperfections or incomplete details emerge. Suddenly, you find yourself back at square one, contemplating another round of renovations or fixes.

This cycle is a common narrative for many homeowners, highlighting the need for a reliable guide and partner in the home improvement journey. It just goes to show you would be wise to seek a different approach to secure the best value for money in a market known for its rapid price variations and the challenge of finding trustworthy contractors. This is where strategic insights and dependable guidance become invaluable, helping you break free from the Homeowner's Hamster Wheel.

Which is why I'm glad you're reading this book. As you turn the page and start reading, you will finally discover the strategies and insights that you've been searching for. This knowledge will empower you to navigate the complexities of home improvement with confidence, ensuring your next project is not just a fleeting success but a lasting enhancement to your home.

# INTRODUCTION

Imagine stepping into your home feeling an overwhelming sense of pride and accomplishment. Your home, a place once mere bricks and mortar, now transformed into a stunning reflection of your personality and lifestyle. It's not just about the extra square footage; it's about enhancing the quality of your life in every way imaginable. That's what strategic home improvements can achieve, and it's within your grasp.

Why should you consider unlocking the potential of your home right now? Well, think about the satisfaction of creating a space that perfectly suits your evolving needs without the hassle of moving. Whether it's adapting to the growing needs of your family, crafting that perfect workspace for your ventures, or simply enhancing your living environment, the reasons are as unique as you are.

Unleashing Possibilities

Every homeowner holds a powerful key – the potential to transform their existing space into something extraordinary. It's not just about adding value in monetary terms, though that is certainly a welcome benefit. It's about reimagining your daily environment so that it aligns with your dreams and aspirations. Your home can be more than just a place to live; it can be a source of inspiration, comfort, and joy.

Taking the first step might seem daunting. You may wonder if it's the right time, question the financial investment, or feel overwhelmed by the sheer scope of planning and executing renovations. However, remember that the most significant changes in our lives often begin with a single brave decision. By choosing to enhance your home, you're not just altering your immediate surroundings – you're setting the stage for a richer, more fulfilling life.

## The Art of Transformation

This book isn't just a guide; it's a journey through the possibilities housed within your existing walls. From loft conversions that open up dark, unused spaces to the charm of elegantly integrated extensions that seemlessly blend the old with the new, each chapter is designed to inspire and inform. Imagine converting that cluttered garage into a vibrant home office, or expanding your living space with a two-storey extension that provides room for both work and play.

The beauty of this journey lies in its customization. You don't need to follow every idea or suggestion. Instead, use these chapters as a springboard for your creativity. Let them guide you through the practical steps while encouraging you to envision and enact changes that resonate with your personal vision.

## Choosing Your Companions

No transformation journey is solitary. The road to renovating your home is paved with critical choices, not least of which is selecting the right people to bring along. Contractors and craftsmen, like those at Prime Joinery, become your partners in this venture. Their expertise can steer your project around common pitfalls and help translate your vision into reality.

In these pages, you'll find essential tips on choosing the right contractor – one who understands your vision, communicates transparently, and respects your budget. Speaking of budget, that's another companion on your journey. A well-planned budget is your roadmap, ensuring that your home improvement adventure does not lead you into financial distress.

## Managing the Magic

As you delve deeper into the book, you'll uncover the secrets to effectively managing your home improvement project. From initial designs and permits to the final touches that make your space unique, every stage of the process is crucial. We'll explore how to keep your project on track and ensure that every decision aligns with your ultimate goals: enhancing your life quality and increasing your home's value.

## The Reward

Finally, imagine the moment when the dust has settled, and you step back to behold your transformed home. This isn't just about enjoying the new features or the additional space. It's about experiencing the profound satisfaction of having created a home that truly reflects who you are and what you love. It's about the smiles of family and friends as they enjoy the new environment you've created. It's about knowing that every decision, every investment, and every small change was part of crafting your ideal living space.

## Your Invitation

So, take this book as your invitation to embark on one of the most rewarding journeys of your life. Whether you're looking to upgrade your living space, increase your property's value, or simply bring a long-held dream to life, you hold the power to make it happen. With each page turn, let yourself be inspired, educated, and motivated to transform your house into your dream home.

Welcome to "Prime Property: Extend, Convert, Renate - A Homeowner's Guide to Strategic Home Improvements." Let's begin this transformative journey together.

#  1

# UNLOCKING YOUR HOME'S POTENTIAL: WHY START NOW?

*"An investment in knowledge pays the best interest."*
 *– Benjamin Franklin*

## The Value of Timely Renovations

Embarking on home renovations can sometimes feel like setting sail on the high seas. It's an adventure that promises new horizons but also requires careful navigation. The fact that you're considering whether to renovate now indicates you're already at the helm, ready to chart a course that enhances your living space and potentially, the value of your property. Let's delve into why timing these renovations aptly can be a game-changer for your home and lifestyle.

## Increasing Property Value

First off, one of the most compelling reasons to grab that contractor's number and get the ball rolling is the potential increase in your home's market value. Renovations, particularly those that enhance the functionality and aesthetic appeal of your home, can significantly boost its worth. But not all renovations are created equal in the eyes of future buyers or appraisers.

The kitchen and bathrooms, for instance, are prime targets for upgrades that pay off. A well-executed kitchen remodel can recoup a substantial percentage of the cost in the value it adds to your home. It's about more than just splashing on a new coat of paint; think about upgrading appliances to modern, energy-efficient models, replacing countertops, or reconfiguring the layout to improve flow and usability.

Bathrooms are another hotspot. Updating fixtures, improving lighting, and adding modern amenities like heated floors can turn ordinary into a selling point. Furthermore, expanding or adding bathrooms can significantly increase your home's appeal and functionality, making it more attractive to potential buyers.

However, it's not just about choosing the right projects. Timing these renovations can impact their value-add too. For instance, updating your heating system or roof just before selling can be a powerful selling point, reassuring potential buyers they won't face immediate, costly repairs.

## Adapting to Lifestyle Changes

Your home needs to evolve with your life. Perhaps you've welcomed a new member to the family, started to work from home, or entered retirement. Each of these life stages can significantly alter what you need from your home.

When the kids come along, space and safety become paramount. Converting an attic into a bedroom or playroom or turning that unused office into a nursery makes your home more suited to a growing family without the need to move. As you transition to working from home, creating a dedicated office space can enhance productivity and help maintain a healthy work-life balance. For those stepping into retirement, modifications might include adding a downstairs bedroom or renovating the bathroom to include accessibility features.

Timely renovations in response to these changes can not only make your daily life more comfortable but can also prevent the stress of a rushed renovation down the line. Plus, by adapting your home to fit your needs as they evolve, you maintain its usability and enjoyment, which is priceless.

## Energy Efficiency Improvements

With rising energy costs and growing environmental concerns, improving your home's energy efficiency is both a financially and socially responsible decision. Initiatives like installing double-glazed windows, upgrading insulation, or switching to a more efficient heating system reduce your energy consumption and can save you a significant amount on bills in the long run.

Moreover, energy-efficient homes are increasingly attractive to buyers if you're considering selling in the future. Many people are looking for homes that will keep operational costs down without requiring immediate upgrades. By implementing these changes now, you can enjoy the cost savings while you're still in the home and potentially benefit from a higher sale price when you decide to move on.

Timing is crucial when it comes to energy improvements. For instance, it might be most cost-effective to replace windows or a boiler during a larger renovation project to minimise disruption and combine costs. Planning these upgrades during off-peak seasons for contractors can also result in better deals and quicker project timelines.

In conclusion, whether it's boosting your home's market value, moulding your living space to better suit your current lifestyle, or cutting down on utility bills through smarter energy use, timely renovations can significantly enhance both the tangible and intangible qualities of your home. Each plank of wood nailed, each stroke of paint applied, is an investment not just in your property but in your life quality. The question isn't just why start now, but rather, why wait? With careful planning and strategic improvements, your home can become more comfortable, stylish, and efficient, all the while preparing for whatever the future holds.

## Assessing Your Needs and Goals

When considering renovations, it's critical to dig deep and understand exactly what you need from your living space. This isn't just about sprucing up; it's about aligning your environment with your lifestyle and looking ahead. Let's break it down into space requirements, personal style, and long-term planning.

Space Requirements

First off, think about how much space you really need. This might sound straightforward, but it's easy to underestimate or overestimate. Start by evaluating your current situation. Are there rooms in your house that are barely used? Or are you constantly bumping into furniture and wishing for a few extra square metres?

Consider your family dynamics as they are now and how they might change. If you're planning to have children, or expecting elderly parents to move in with you in the future, your space needs could look quite different in a few years. Flexible spaces that can evolve as your needs change, such as convertible home offices or bedrooms, might be particularly valuable.

It's also worth considering the 'flow' of your home. How do the rooms connect with each other? Is there a logical progression from one space to another? Creating a sense of flow can make your home feel larger and more cohesive, even without adding extra square footage. Sometimes, knocking down a non-structural wall or adding doors where walls once were can completely transform how a space feels and functions.

Personal Style

Moving to personal style, this is your chance to make your mark. Your home should reflect who you are, but remember, renovating for flashy trends might not appeal to you or potential buyers a few years down the line. Instead, focus on timeless style that resonates with your personal aesthetics.

Think about colours, textures, and materials. Do you lean towards the warm, earthy tones, or do you prefer a sleek, modern look with sharp lines and high contrast? This isn't just about beauty; it's about creating environments that make you feel good. For instance, using natural wood can evoke warmth and comfort, perfect for family rooms or bedrooms.

However, personal style isn't just about the visual. It's also about functionality. You might love the look of a minimalist home, but if you have three kids and a dog, maintaining a pristine environment can be more stressful than it's worth. Choose finishes and furnishings that are not only beautiful but also durable and easy to clean.

## Long-term Planning

Finally, let's talk about long-term planning. Renovations can be costly and disruptive, so it makes sense to think long-term to make sure you're creating a home that you can grow into, rather than out of. Consider your future in the home. Are you renovating to sell, or do you see yourself staying put for decades?

If you're planning to sell, consider what improvements are most likely to increase your home's value and appeal to potential buyers. Kitchen and bathroom updates usually offer the best return on investment. Adding an extra bathroom or updating an old one can make a significant difference in your home's marketability and functionality.

On the other hand, if you're planning to stay, think about what will make your life more comfortable day-to-day. Maybe that's energy-efficient appliances that can save money in the long run, or perhaps it's as simple as adding more natural light with skylights or larger windows.

Also, consider the sustainability of your renovations. Using high-quality materials that are durable and energy-efficient can reduce maintenance costs and help your home stand the test of time. Plus, sustainable homes are increasingly in demand, which could be a significant advantage if the market changes and you eventually decide to sell.

In summary, assessing your needs and goals before diving

into home renovations is more than just a preliminary step; it's a crucial part of ensuring that your investment pays off in comfort, style, and financial returns. Take the time to really think about what you need, what you love, and where you see yourself in the future. This strategic approach will not only transform your property but also enhance your lifestyle.

## Understanding the Basics of Home Alterations

When you're considering making changes to your home, it's essential to grasp the different types of alterations available, the common challenges you might face, and the legal considerations to keep in mind. Let's dive into each of these areas to ensure you're well-prepared for your home improvement journey.

## Types of Alterations

Home alterations can range from minor tweaks to major renovations, and understanding the scope of what's possible can help you make informed decisions. Typically, alterations fall into one of three categories: structural, cosmetic, and extensions.

**1.Structural Alterations:** These are changes to the core elements of your home. Think about removing or altering load-bearing walls, modifying the roof, or changing the layout of your home to create an open-plan living area. Structural changes are complex and usually require professional design services and building approvals.

**2.Cosmetic Alterations:** These improvements are all about aesthetics. Painting walls, updating fixtures, and replacing flooring fall into this category. Cosmetic alterations can dramatically improve the look and feel of your space without altering the fundamental structure of the building.

**3.Extensions:** Need more space? Extensions add square footage to your home. Whether it's pushing out a wall to expand your kitchen or adding an entirely new room, extensions can significantly increase your living area and potentially boost your property value. Like structural alterations, extensions often require planning permission and should comply with local building codes.

Each type of alteration serves different purposes and comes with its own set of considerations. Whether you're looking to enhance functionality or increase your home's market appeal, aligning the type of work you undertake with your long-term objectives is crucial.

## Common Challenges

Embarking on home alterations isn't without its hurdles. Anticipating these challenges can help you manage the renovation process more effectively.

**1. Budget Overruns:** Even the best-planned projects can end up costing more than expected. Unexpected structural issues, changes to the project scope, and choice of materials can all impact your budget. To mitigate this, it's wise to have a contingency fund of at least 10-20% of your total budget.

**2. Time Delays:** Home improvement projects are notorious for taking longer than planned. Weather conditions, delays in materials delivery, and unforeseen structural problems can all push back your timeline. Flexibility and patience are key, as well as regular communication with your contractors.

**3. Living Disruptions:** Depending on the scale of your alterations, you might have to live in a construction zone for a while. Dust, noise, and workers coming in and out of your home can disrupt your daily life. If the project is extensive, you might even need to consider temporary accommodation.

**4. Quality Control:** Maintaining high standards throughout the renovation process is essential. This can be challenging if you're not regularly on-site to oversee the work. Hiring reliable, skilled professionals and establishing clear lines of communication from the start can help ensure that the work meets your expectations.

## Legal Considerations

Before you pick up a hammer or tear down a wall, it's crucial to understand the legal landscape surrounding home alterations.

**1.Planning Permissions:** Depending on where you live and what type of alterations you're planning, you may need to get planning permission from your local council. This is especially true for extensions and major structural changes. Check with your local planning authority to understand the specific requirements for your project.

**2.Building Regulations:** These are standards for designing and constructing buildings to ensure the safety and health for the people who use those buildings. They cover everything from fire safety to energy efficiency. Failure to comply can result in fines and having to redo the work.

**3.Neighbour Considerations:** Under the Party Wall etc. Act1996, you must notify your neighbours if you plan to carry out any construction work near or on your shared property boundary, or 'party wall'. This is to prevent any disputes that might arise due to misunderstandings or damage.

Understanding these basics of home alterations not only helps in achieving a smoother renovation process but also ensures that the improvements you make are legal, sustainable, and beneficial in the long run. Whether you're renovating to sell or to build your dream home, getting these foundational aspects right is crucial.

## RECAP AND ACTION ITEMS

Congratulations on taking the first steps towards unlocking your home's potential. By now, you've explored the value of timely renovations, assessed your personal needs and goals, and grasped the basics of home alterations. Let's cement what you've learned with some practical action steps that will propel you forward in your home improvement journey.

**1. Evaluate Your Home's Current Value:** Before you swing a hammer, it's crucial to understand your property's current market value and how much value potential improvements could add. Consider consulting with a local estate agent or a property valuer to get an accurate picture.

**2. Prioritise Adaptability:** As your life evolves, so do your living needs. Reflect on how your current space might need to change to accommodate new circumstances like remote working or expanding your family. This foresight can save you from future costly re-renovations.

**3. Audit Your Energy Usage:** Energy efficiency is not just good for the planet—it's great for your wallet too. Have an energy audit conducted to see where you could make impactful changes, such as upgrading insulation or installing energy-efficient windows.

**4. Space Planning:** Now that you understand your space requirements, sketch out a rough plan of your desired alterations. Use this as a guide to discuss with architects or builders to see what's feasible within your budget and space constraints.

**5.Define Your Style:** Gather inspiration for your home's new look. Whether it's browsing through design magazines, creating mood boards on Pinterest, or visiting showrooms, getting a clear visual idea of your personal style will help guide your renovation choices.

**6.Long-Term Vision:** Think about where you see yourself in the next 5-10 years and how your home fits into that picture. This long-term planning can influence decisions like whether to add an extension, convert a loft, or renovate existing rooms.

**7.Understand Legalities:** Before proceeding with any work, make sure you're clear on the legal requirements. Check if you need planning permission for your intended alterations or if there are any building regulations you need to comply with.

**8.Choose the Right Contractors:** The success of your renovation greatly depends on the people you hire. Take your time to select experienced, reputable contractors who come highly recommended. Always get multiple quotes and check references.

By following these steps, you're not just renovating your home; you're strategically enhancing your lifestyle and investment. Take action today, and transform your home into a place that not only looks great but also works perfectly for your future. Happy renovating!

# 2

# LOFT CONVERSIONS: MAXIMIZING SPACE CREATIVELY

*"Space is the breath of art."*
— *Frank Lloyd Wright*

Planning Your Loft Conversion

When embarking on the adventurous journey of converting your loft, the excitement can barely be contained. However, before you let your imagination run wild with design ideas, it's crucial to lay a solid foundation for your project. Planning your loft conversion involves a trifecta of essential steps: evaluating space and potential, considering the design, and understanding building regulations. Let's dive into these aspects to ensure your loft conversion is not only beautiful but also practical and compliant.

## Evaluating Space and Potential

First things first, you need to assess what you're working with. This initial evaluation will determine the feasibility of your loft conversion and help shape your expectations realistically. Start by examining the structure of your existing loft space. Key elements to consider include the roof structure, the head height, and the footprint of the loft. Traditional cut and pitched roofs are often easier to convert due to their spacious triangular shapes, whereas modern truss sectioned roofs might require more structural reinforcement, thus increasing the complexity and cost.

Head height is a critical factor; a minimum height of 2.2 meters is generally required to provide comfortable living space. Measure from the top of the ceiling joist to underneath the ridgeboard in the apex. If the head height is lacking, don't get discouraged. Solutions like raising the roof or lowering the ceiling of the floor below can be explored, although these will need more substantial structural work and of course, a larger budget.

The footprint of your loft also determines the possible layout and functionality of the space. Larger footprints allow for more flexibility in terms of design and utility. Can it accommodate the extra bathroom you need, or perhaps that quiet home office away from the daily bustle? Once you've assessed these elements, you'll have a clearer picture of what type of conversion is possible and how you can utilise this new space effectively.

## Design Considerations

Moving onto the fun part – designing your new space! This is where you can inject your personality and style into the loft conversion. However, remember that good design is not just about aesthetics but also about functionality. Start by considering the purpose of the converted loft. Whether it's a bedroom, playroom, study, or something else, the function will heavily influence the design elements.

Think about the flow of the space. Where will the stairs go? How will they integrate with the current layout of your home? Stairs that are too steep or awkwardly placed can be a hazard and can disrupt the flow of your house. Also, consider the placement of windows and skylights, which are crucial for natural light and ventilation, enhancing both the ambiance and the energy efficiency of your loft.

Thermal and acoustic insulation are other key design considerations that can greatly impact the comfort of your loft conversion. Proper insulation will help stabilise temperatures, keep out external noise, and reduce heating bills. Lastly, don't forget about the interior design. Selecting the right colours, materials, and finishes can transform the feel of the space. Light colours and strategically placed mirrors, for example, can make small spaces feel larger and more open.

## Building Regulations

Now, onto the nitty-gritty: building regulations. Navigating through these can be less thrilling, but they are crucial for ensuring your loft conversion is safe, secure, and legally compliant. Building regulations cover a range of criteria including fire safety, insulation, soundproofing, and stairs accessibility. You'll need to ensure that the converted loft has a safe means of escape in case of fire and that it is accessible without compromising any existing escape routes from other parts of the house.

You should also consider the Party Wall Act if the work involves altering a wall that you share with neighbours. It's always a good idea to have a friendly chat with them before you start the project to keep everything cordial and transparent. Hiring a professional to help navigate these regulations can be a smart move. A good architect or building surveyor will not only help ensure compliance but can also suggest ways to creatively meet these standards without compromising your design.

Remember, while the planning stage might seem daunting, thorough preparation is key to the success of your loft conversion. Take the time to evaluate your space's potential, design thoughtfully, and understand the legal requirements. By doing so, you set the stage for a smooth and successful transformation of your loft space.

# The Construction Process

Step-by-step guide

Embarking on a loft conversion is a bit like piecing together an intricate jigsaw puzzle where every component must align perfectly. Let's break down the steps so you can visualise the process and ensure every piece falls into place.

Firstly, once your plans are drawn up and permissions secured, the initial stage involves preparing your loft. This might mean clearing out old belongings, which can be quite the trip down memory lane but remember, the aim is to maximise space. The loft then needs to be assessed for any pre-existing issues like leaks or insulation deficits, which should be addressed before the heavy lifting starts.

Next up, structural strengthening is crucial. Depending on the design, this could involve reinforcing the floor joists to support additional weight. This stage is not just about laying down new beams but ensuring they integrate seamlessly with your home's current structure - think of it as the skeleton of your project that everything else will build on.

With the structure secure, the installation of dormer windows or skylights is typically next. Not only do these enhance the aesthetic appeal, but they are essential for natural light and ventilation. It's a transformative step that suddenly turns a dark attic into a bright, airy space.

Following this, the roof is insulated and made weatherproof. In the UK, where the weather can be unforgiving, ensuring your loft is snug and dry throughout the year is non-negotiable. It's crucial to choose high-quality materials for insulation to meet the regulatory standards and also to future-proof your home against energy losses.

The construction of internal walls and the installation of utilities come next. Plumbing, electrical wiring, and heating systems are extended from the main part of your house into the loft. Precision here is key; faulty wiring or plumbing can lead to disasters, so it's crucial these are handled by certified professionals.

Finally, plastering and the initial stages of decoration begin. Once the plaster dries, you'll really start to see your new space taking shape, looking less like a construction site and more like part of your home.

## Timing and phases

Understanding the timeline and planning for each phase of your loft conversion project can significantly reduce stress and help manage expectations. Typically, a loft conversion can take anywhere from8 to12 weeks, depending on the complexity and scale of the project.

The preparatory work often moves swiftly; however, the structural changes can vary in time. It's wise to factor in some buffer time for unexpected challenges. Weather conditions can play a significant role in how quickly external work progresses, especially with tasks like roof modifications.

Utilities and internal fittings might need coordination with various professionals whose schedules could be tight. Organising this in advance and maintaining clear, ongoing communication can help in keeping this phase as streamlined as possible.

Each stage of the process will have its mini-milestones, and seeing these come to fruition can be quite satisfying. Keep a checklist and maintain regular contact with your contractor to ensure that you remain in sync with the project timeline.

## Handling disruptions

Let's face it, construction is messy and disruptive. However, with some clever strategies, you can mitigate the chaos and maintain a semblance of normalcy.

Firstly, consider your living arrangements during the construction. If the work is extensive and the intrusion too disruptive, it might be worth temporarily relocating. If staying put is more your thing, set up clear barriers to dust and noise. Temporary partitions or plastic sheeting can be effective in keeping the rest of your house clean and quiet.

Communicate with your builders about your daily routine and establish clear boundaries and work hours. This helps in minimising disruption during your personal or family time. It's also beneficial to inform your neighbours about the project timeline. Keeping them in the loop can help ease any potential tensions caused by unexpected noise or disruptions.

Lastly, maintaining a sense of humour is essential. Construction can be full of surprises, and things might not always go according to plan. A flexible attitude will help you handle bumps along the road more smoothly and keep the project enjoyable rather than stressful.

By breaking down the construction process into these comprehensive steps, timing the phases accurately, and handling disruptions with grace, your journey from dusty attic to dazzling loft conversion will be as seamless as possible. Remember, each phase brings you closer to realising your vision - transforming unused space into your dream room.

## Finishing Touches

Once the dust has settled, and the construction noise has dwindled, you're stepping into the most thrilling phase of your loft conversion journey. It's time to infuse your newly carved space with personality and practicality. Here, we'll dive into interior design tips, clever storage solutions, and the essentials of lighting and ventilation. These elements will transform your loft from a mere structural addition into a vibrant and functional living space.

## Interior Design Tips

Designing the interior of your loft can be as exhilarating as it is daunting. You're presented with a blank canvas, albeit sometimes with quirky angles and sloped ceilings typical of loft spaces. Here's how to tackle this wonderfully unique challenge.

Firstly, embrace the quirks. Those sloped ceilings and odd corners are what give your loft its character. Use these features to create cosy nooks or dramatic design statements. For instance, a low corner can perfectly house a built-in reading nook complete with plush cushions and ample lighting.

Speaking of light, colour plays a pivotal role in how spacious your loft feels. Light hues make rooms feel bigger and airier, which is essential in attic spaces that can feel cramped. Opt for soft shades of blues, greens, or simply a crisp white to maximise the sense of space. If you're a fan of wallpaper, consider using it on just one feature wall to avoid overwhelming the space.

When it comes to furniture, choose pieces that are proportional to the size of your loft. Bulky furniture can crowd your loft, making it feel smaller. Opt for multi-functional furniture like ottomans that offer both seating and storage or a sofa bed to accommodate overnight guests. Remember, in a loft, every square inch counts, so opt for sleek, compact pieces that enhance functionality without sacrificing style.

Finally, let your personality shine through with your choice of accessories. Art pieces, rugs, and decorative items are more than just fillers; they're expressions of your style. Use them to inject colour and texture into your loft, making the space truly yours.

## Storage Solutions

Innovative storage solutions are the secret sauce to a clutter-free and spacious loft. Given the unconventional structure of most lofts, traditional storage might not always work. Here's how to think outside the box—literally.

First, consider built-in storage. Custom shelves and drawers can be tailored to fit into awkward spaces under the eaves or along sloping walls, making use of areas that might otherwise go wasted. These built-ins can be designed to blend seamlessly with the walls, maintaining a sleek and uncluttered look.

Don't overlook the potential of the staircase leading up to your loft. The space beneath each step can be transformed into drawers or shelves, perfect for storing everything from books to seasonal clothing. This not only maximises space but also keeps your belongings neatly organised and easily accessible.

Another clever storage idea is to utilise vertical space. High shelves, for example, can be installed right up to the ceiling, drawing the eye upwards and making the room feel larger. Just ensure you have a sturdy ladder or a stylish stepping stool handy for access.

Freestanding storage units can also work wonders, especially if they're on wheels. These can be moved around as needed, offering flexibility in how you use your space. Plus, they can be taken with you if you move, offering a versatile and investment-worthy storage solution.

## Lighting and Ventilation

The right lighting and ventilation are crucial for making your loft a comfortable, breathable space. Poorly lit or stuffy lofts are far from inviting, but with the right approach, you can ensure yours is both bright and airy.

Start with natural light. If possible, maximise the amount of daylight that enters your loft. Skylights are particularly effective as they bring in an abundance of natural light and can be opened to improve air circulation. They also don't take up valuable wall space, which can be used for storage or as an art display.

Artificial lighting should be layered to create the right mood and functionality. Ambient lighting can be achieved with ceiling-mounted fixtures, while task lighting is crucial in areas like reading nooks or office spaces. Don't forget accent lighting; small, directed lights can highlight architectural features or artworks, adding depth and dimension to the room.

Ventilation is equally important. Good airflow is essential to prevent your loft from becoming stuffy, especially during warmer months. Consider integrating a ventilation system during the planning phase of your conversion. For a cost-effective solution, ensure windows are operable and consider adding vents to help promote cross ventilation.

By focusing on these three key areas in the final phase of your loft conversion, you ensure not just the functionality of your space but also its comfort and appeal. Whether you're looking for a quiet retreat under the eaves or a vibrant family room in the sky, your loft can provide that much-needed additional space tailored precisely to your needs.

## RECAP AND ACTION ITEMS

Congratulations! You've navigated through the comprehensive journey of planning, constructing, and finalising your loft conversion. You are now equipped with the essential knowledge to transform that underutilised space at the top of your house into a vibrant and functional area. Let's recap the key takeaways and outline some actionable steps to propel you forward.

Firstly, you assessed the potential of your loft space, considering its dimensions and structural integrity. You also delved into the design aspects, ensuring the layout suits your lifestyle while adhering to the necessary building regulations. These initial steps set a solid foundation for your project, aligning your vision with practical possibilities.

Moving into the construction phase, you followed a step-by-step guide to bring this vision to life. You've learned how to pace the project through various stages, managing time effectively to minimise disruption to your daily life. Remember, the smoother the process, the quicker you'll enjoy your new space.

Finally, you've applied the finishing touches that transform the structure into your personal haven. Through clever interior design, you've maximised every inch of the room, integrating storage solutions that maintain a clutter-free environment. The choices in lighting and ventilation not only enhance functionality but also ensure that your loft is a comfortable, airy space.

**ACTION ITEMS:**

**1. Review the Plans:** Revisit your design and planning documents one last time to ensure everything is in line with your goals and compliance requirements

**2. Schedule Consultations:** If you haven't already, now is the time to book consultations with any additional professionals such as interior designers or lighting experts

**3. Create a Timeline:** Draft a detailed timeline or checklist for the construction phase if you haven't done so. Include buffer periods for unforeseen delays to keep your project on track

**4. Plan for Disruptions:** Prepare your household for the upcoming construction work. It might be arranging alternative storage for your belongings or setting up temporary living arrangements if necessary

**5. Shopping List:** Make a comprehensive list of all fixtures, fittings, and furniture you need to purchase. Prioritise items based on their delivery and installation times

**6. Celebrate Milestones:** Keep morale high by celebrating small milestones. Completed the framing? Have a small celebration. It helps keep the momentum going.

By following these steps, you are not just renovating a space; you are enhancing your living environment and potentially increasing your property's value. Dive into this project with enthusiasm and watch as your loft transforms into one of the best places in your home. Happy converting!

# 3

# EXPANDING OUTWARDS: SINGLE STOREY EXTENSIONS

*"Make your home as comfortable and attractive as possible and then get on with living. There's more to life than decorating."*
— *Albert Hadley*

## Designing for Harmony and Function

When embarking on the journey of adding a single-storey extension to your home, the blend of aesthetics and practicality can't be overstated. It's not just about creating more space; it's about enhancing the flow and feel of your existing home to achieve a seamless union of the old and the new. Let's dive into how you can achieve this harmony and functionality through thoughtful design, meticulous material selection, and prioritising accessibility.

## Integration with Existing Structures

The magic happens when your new extension looks like it was always meant to be there. To start, consider the architectural style of your existing home. Is it modern with minimalist lines, or is it a period property brimming with character? Your extension should echo these themes to create a cohesive look.

Visual continuity is key. Pay attention to roof lines; if your home features a pitched roof, carrying this design element into your extension can help merge the two structures gracefully. Windows and doors are another area where matching or complementing styles will help in blending the new with the old. For example, if your original home has bay windows, incorporating similar shapes or styles can help unify the appearance.

Next, think about the proportions of your extension in relation to your existing home. An extension that is too large might overshadow your original building, while something too small may look like an afterthought. Aim for a balance that feels intentional and proportionate.

Lastly, consider the sight lines from within and around your home. Your extension should enhance, not obstruct, views from existing windows and doors. It should also create inviting perspectives and vistas that draw the eye seamlessly from the old part of your home into the new.

## Material Selection

Choosing the right materials is pivotal not only for design harmony but also for the longevity and performance of your extension. Material choices should complement the existing home, respecting its character while also ensuring durability.

Brickwork can be matched or contrasted tastefully. For a harmonious effect, source bricks that match those used in your original home in colour, size, and texture. If a direct match isn't possible, consider a complementary colour palette that blends well with the existing masonry.

For a more modern twist, materials like glass, steel, or timber can be used to provide a contemporary contrast that still respects the overall aesthetic of the site. Large glass panels can bring a modern edge to a traditional home, offering the added benefit of enhancing natural light within the extension.

The roof and flooring are other areas where material choice impacts both aesthetics and function. Roof materials should ideally match or complement what's on your existing home. Inside, flooring should offer a smooth transition between old and new spaces. If you have wooden floors in the original structure, continuing this material into your extension can enhance the sense of continuity.

## Accessibility Considerations

An often overlooked but critical aspect of designing an extension is ensuring it is accessible. This means thinking about how people of all ages and abilities will interact with the space.

Begin with the entrance to the extension. Are there steps? Could these be a barrier for someone with mobility issues? Consider installing ramps or designing the extension level with the rest of your house to promote ease of access.

Inside, think about door widths and thresholds. A wider doorway accommodates everyone from delivery people with large packages to individuals using mobility aids. Flush thresholds can prevent trips and are easier for wheelchair users to navigate.

In terms of layout, open-plan designs can be very accessible. They allow for more flexible furniture arrangements and clear movement paths. However, ensure there is ample room to manoeuvre around furniture comfortably for those with mobility aids.

Light switches, power sockets, and other controls should be placed at reachable heights for all users. Consider smart home technology for lights, heating, and blinds to provide an additional layer of accessibility.

Incorporating these elements from the start of your design process means your extension won't just be a beautiful space but a functional one that enhances the quality of life for everyone in your home.

By addressing these key aspects — integration with existing structures, material selection, and accessibility considerations — your single-storey extension will not only meet your needs but also complement and enhance the overall character and functionality of your home.

## Practical Construction Insights

### Foundation Requirements

When you're expanding your home with a single storey extension, the foundation isn't just the starting point of your project; it's the bedrock that determines the durability and safety of your extended space. Think of it as the base of a tree, where stability is paramount. Before you get swept away with the aesthetic aspects, understanding the technicalities of foundation work is essential.

Firstly, assess the type of soil on your property. Different soil types, from clay to sand, affect how you should approach the foundation. Clay, for instance, expands and contracts significantly with moisture levels, which can lead to structural problems if not accounted for. In contrast, sandy soils offer better drainage but might lack the stability needed without deeper, more robust foundations.

The depth and type of foundation you choose depend heavily on these soil characteristics. For most single storey extensions, strip foundations—where a continuous strip of concrete is laid below all load-bearing walls—are common. However, in areas with problematic soils, you might need to consider pile foundations, where deep holes are drilled and filled with concrete to anchor the structure securely.

Additionally, don't overlook the existing foundation of your home. The new extension must integrate seamlessly with it to avoid differential settlement – where different parts of the building settle unevenly, potentially causing cracks and structural issues. Hiring a skilled structural engineer can provide you with peace of mind, ensuring that your foundation supports not just the new extension, but harmonises with the whole building.

## Weather Considerations

The British weather can be unforgiving, and when constructing an extension, it pays to consider how the elements might impact your build. Planning construction phases around weather forecasts can save you not only frustration but also time and money.

Start with the roofing and waterproofing processes. These should be scheduled during drier periods. Water can wreak havoc on building materials and slow down the construction process significantly. For instance, laying the foundation and external walls during a wet season might lead to waterlogging, which compromises the strength of the concrete and the drying time.

Moreover, consider how your extension will cope with seasonal changes. Features like overhangs or awnings can protect your walls from rainwater, while well-planned guttering can prevent issues with water pooling around the base of your structure.

Thermal movement is another weather-related factor to consider. Materials expand and contract depending on the temperature. For example, using materials like timber, which has a higher rate of expansion, might require you to plan for small gaps or flexible joints to accommodate this movement.

## Insulation and Energy Efficiency

Energy efficiency is not just a buzzword; it's a practical strategy to reduce heating bills and increase comfort in your home. When planning your extension, think of insulation as a thermal envelope that wraps around your new space, keeping it warm in the winter and cool in the summer.

The walls, floor, and roof of your extension are all critical areas to insulate properly. Using high-performance materials like PIR (polyisocyanurate) boards can make a significant difference. These are not only highly effective but also thin, saving precious internal space. For floors, consider rigid insulation panels, which can be laid beneath concrete floor slabs to prevent heat loss.

Windows and doors are also crucial in the insulation equation. Double-glazing or even triple-glazing can be beneficial. These not only insulate but also reduce noise pollution—an added bonus if your home is in a busy area.

Incorporating renewable energy sources can further enhance your home's energy efficiency. Solutions like solar panels or air source heat pumps might represent an upfront cost but can lead to substantial energy savings in the long term. Furthermore, these additions can increase the value of your home, making them a worthwhile consideration for both your comfort and investment potential.

By integrating these practical construction insights into your project, you ensure that your single storey extension is built on a solid foundation, capable of withstanding the elements and providing energy efficiency for years to come. Remember, the quality of construction not only affects your immediate living environment but also the long-term value and safety of your home.

## Interior and Exterior Finishing

When it comes to single-storey extensions, the magic really happens in the finishing touches. The choices you make for the interior and exterior finishing can dramatically affect the overall look and feel of your new space. Here, we will guide you through flooring options, external aesthetics, and landscaping integration, ensuring that every detail contributes positively to your home.

## Flooring Options

Selecting the right flooring for your extension is crucial not just for aesthetics but also for functionality and durability. The type of flooring you choose should seamlessly integrate with existing floors while also meeting the specific needs of the new space.

**1.Continuity with Existing Flooring:** If your extension is an open plan that connects with other parts of the house, you might want to consider continuing the same flooring to create a sense of unity and flow. This could mean extending hardwood, tiles, or whatever material is predominant in your existing home. However, if a perfect match isn't possible due to discontinuation of your existing flooring or budget constraints, finding a complementary style or colour can work just as well.

**2.Functionality:** Consider the primary use of the extension. Is it going to be a kitchen, a living space, or perhaps a utility room? Kitchens and utility areas benefit from more resilient and easy-to-clean flooring like ceramic tiles or vinyl, which can handle moisture and stains better than hardwood or carpet. Living spaces, meanwhile, might call for something warmer and more inviting like engineered wood or a plush carpet.

**3. Underfloor Heating:** If you're adding underfloor heating, certain flooring options are better conductors of heat than others. Stone and ceramic tiles work excellently with underfloor heating systems due to their thermal conducting properties, ensuring the room is evenly heated. Wooden floors can also be used, but you'll need to ensure they are suitable for high heat conditions and won't warp over time.

## External Aesthetics

The exterior look of your extension is just as important as the inside. It's the first thing people see and it sets the tone for their expectations of the rest of your home.

**1. Matching the Existing Structure:** To achieve a cohesive look, your extension should complement the architectural style and materials of the existing house. This doesn't mean you have to use the exact same materials, but they should harmonise. For example, if your house is brick, you might consider a rendered finish with a colour that matches or contrasts beautifully with the brick.

**2. Windows and Doors:** Choosing the right windows and doors can also impact the overall aesthetic. Larger windows not only bring in more natural light but can make the extension feel more spacious and integrated with the outdoors. Bi-fold or sliding doors can open up a room to the garden, enhancing both the utility and beauty of the extension.

**3.Colour Scheme:** The colour of the exterior walls should either match or pleasantly contrast with the main house. Neutral colours are generally a safe choice as they blend well with various materials and styles. However, don't be afraid to use bolder colours if it suits the character of your home and neighbourhood.

## Landscaping Integration

The way your extension interacts with your garden and outdoor space can significantly influence its success. Thoughtful landscaping can help blend the new structure into the environment and enhance its appearance.

**1.Creating a Seamless Transition:** If your extension includes doors opening out onto a garden, consider how the design of your garden can create a smooth transition. Decking that extends from inside to outside, for example, can effectively blur the boundaries between the two spaces. Similarly, patios or terraces that match the interior flooring can extend the living space outdoors.

**2.Planting Choices:** Strategic planting can also help integrate your extension into the garden. Consider using shrubs and small trees to soften the edges of the building or to hide any less appealing aspects like drainage or foundations. Climbers or trailing plants can also be used to help the new structure meld with the old.

**3. Lighting:** Don't forget about outdoor lighting, which can enhance not only the usability of your external space in the evenings but also the overall aesthetic appeal. Subtle garden lighting can highlight key features and plants, while architectural lighting can accentuate the design elements of your extension.

By carefully considering each of these elements, you ensure that your single-storey extension is not only a functional addition to your home but also a beautiful one that enhances its overall value and appeal. Whether it's choosing the right floor, picking harmonious exterior materials, or integrating the landscape design, each decision plays a critical role in transforming your space into a seamless and inviting part of your home.

## RECAP AND ACTION ITEMS

You've just navigated through the essential elements of expanding your home with a single-storey extension. By focusing on designing for harmony and function, addressing practical construction insights, and considering interior and exterior finishing, you're now equipped with a holistic view of the process. Let's consolidate this knowledge into actionable steps to transform these insights into reality.

**1. Design Review:** Take a moment to revisit your design plans. Do they integrate seamlessly with your existing structure? Ensure that the materials selected complement your home's current style while also catering to functional requirements like accessibility. Adjust your plans as needed to achieve both aesthetic and practical harmony.

**2.Consult Professionals:** While the enthusiasm to dive straight into the project might be high, consulting with an architect or a structural engineer can provide you with invaluable insights, especially concerning the foundation requirements and the specific weather considerations for your area. Their expertise will ensure that your extension is not only beautiful but also structurally sound and compliant with local building regulations.

**3.Energy Efficiency:** Re-evaluate your insulation plans and energy efficiency strategies. Could you integrate more sustainable materials or technologies? Perhaps installing triple-glazed windows or upgrading your insulation materials could increase your home's energy efficiency, ultimately saving you money in the long run.

**4.Material Acquisition:** Start sourcing your materials. Keep quality, sustainability, and durability at the forefront of your choices. Remember, the right materials can drastically enhance the longevity and appearance of your extension.

**5.Plan Your Finishes:** Both your interior and exterior finishes should not only look good but also stand the test of time. Choose flooring that offers durability and comfort, and plan your external aesthetics to enhance your home's character.

**6.Landscaping Considerations:** Finally, think about how your extension will transition into your outdoor space. Planning for landscaping early can ensure a smooth flow between your indoor and outdoor environments, making for a stunning visual and functional result.

By following these steps, you are not just extending your home; you are enhancing your living space and potentially increasing your property's value. Remember, the key to a successful home improvement project lies in meticulous planning and execution. So take your time, plan thoroughly, and create a space that you and your family will enjoy for years to come.

# 4

# GOING BIGGER: TWO STOREY EXTENSIONS

*"Make no little plans; they have no magic to stir men's blood."*
*– Daniel Burnham*

## The Double Advantage

When you're contemplating the leap from a single-storey to a two-storey extension, it's like upgrading from a smartphone to the latest smart home system. Both serve fundamental purposes, but the latter brings a whole new level of functionality and flair to your daily life. Let's delve into why scaling up could be a game-changer for your living space.

## Benefits over Single Storey

First off, the obvious – space. A two-storey extension doubles your gain without eating away any more of your precious garden than a single storey would. Imagine what you could do with that extra room. A spacious master suite with a walk-in wardrobe, perhaps? Or maybe a quiet, secluded office away from the hustle and bustle of your household's communal areas? The possibilities stretch as far as your imagination can roam.

But it's not just about the additional square metres. Opting for a two-storey extension can dramatically enhance the resale value of your home. Buyers tend to get more excited about homes that boast optimal living and sleeping spaces, especially in urban areas where space is at a premium. Essentially, you're not just investing in your current lifestyle but in your future financial security as well.

Then there's the aesthetic appeal. A two-storey extension gives you a canvas to redefine the architectural style of your home. Whether you want to complement the existing design or take a bold new direction, this is your chance to make a statement. Plus, with the extra wall space, you can play around with larger windows or striking features like a balcony, which can transform not just the look of your home but also how it interacts with the surrounding environment.

## Structural Considerations

Venturing into the realm of two-storey extensions, however, does bring its complexities, especially regarding structure. The foundation of your existing home plays a pivotal role here. It needs to be robust enough to support the additional weight without compromising the integrity of the entire building. This is where a seasoned structural engineer comes into play. They can assess the current state of your foundations and determine whether reinforcement is needed before any new work begins.

The materials you choose for the build are equally important. They not only have to match or complement your existing structure but also need to adhere to local building regulations. This could affect everything from the height of your extension to the types of materials used, so early consultation with an architect or builder can save you a heap of time and money down the road.

Another aspect often overlooked is the impact of a new extension on the overall balance of your home. Adding a second storey can change the dynamics of how weight is distributed across the building. This might influence everything from the type of roofing you can use to the placement of windows and doors. A thorough analysis by professionals can ensure that your new extension not only looks good but is also structurally sound and functional.

## Balancing Aesthetics

Now, aesthetics — it's not just about what you see inside but also how harmoniously your extension blends with the external character of your home and its surroundings. The last thing you want is for your new addition to stick out like a sore thumb. Achieving this balance is part art, part science.

Firstly, consider the architectural style of your existing home. Is it modern, Victorian, Edwardian, or something else? Your extension should either complement this style or provide a tasteful contrast that enhances the overall appearance of your property. For instance, clean, straight lines and large glass panels might suit a more contemporary home, while brickwork and detailed window frames might be better suited to traditional styles.

The choice of materials can make or break the visual harmony. Natural materials like stone or wood can help integrate the new structure into a rural setting, while more refined materials like glass or steel might be better suited to urban environments. The colour palette also plays a crucial role; it should either match or subtly contrast with the existing building to create a cohesive look.

Finally, consider the visual impact from inside the house as well. The flow between the old and new parts of your home should be seamless, encouraging a natural movement and interaction between spaces. Strategic placement of doors and windows can help achieve this flow, not just by providing practical access points but also by enhancing sightlines and encouraging natural light to flood through your home, making it feel more spacious and connected.

In conclusion, while the journey to adding a two-storey extension to your home involves careful consideration of both structural integrity and aesthetic harmony, the benefits can be immensely rewarding. Not only does it significantly increase your living space without compromising outdoor areas, but it also adds substantial value and character to your property, ensuring that your home not only meets your current needs but also adapts to future demands.

## Technical Execution

### Enhanced Structural Support

When you're planning to go big with a two-storey extension, it's not just about adding more space—it's about doing it safely and sustainably. The structural support of your existing home needs to be evaluated and likely enhanced to carry the additional load of another floor.

First things first, engage a structural engineer. This isn't just a nice-to-have, it's an absolute must. They will assess the current foundation and structure of your home and determine what needs to be beefed up. This might involve underpinning the foundations, which essentially means extending them to bear the extra weight. It's a bit like ensuring your legs are strong enough to carry you if you suddenly had to carry a heavy backpack all day, every day.

The materials you choose for the extension should complement the existing structure but also provide the necessary strength. Steel beams are a popular choice for their robustness and ability to span large openings without support from columns, which is great for open-plan spaces on the ground floor. These beams, coupled with concrete floors, can significantly reduce the sound transmission between floors—a win for both practicality and peace of mind.

Remember, the goal here is not only to support the new upper storey but also to prevent any damage to your existing home. Cracks in walls or a sagging roof are signs that the structure is under stress, so this stage needs careful planning and execution.

## Plumbing and Electrical Adjustments

With an additional floor, you'll need to think about extending your plumbing and electrical systems. It's not just about adding more outlets or a couple of extra taps; it's about ensuring that the system as a whole can handle the increased demand.

For plumbing, consider the water pressure. Your current system may provide sufficient pressure for a single-storey house, but with another level added, the dynamics change. You might need to install a pump or adjust the pressure settings to ensure that your showers on the new top floor aren't just a trickle. Also, think about the drainage – gravity plays a pivotal role here, and you need to ensure that waste water can be effectively carried away from the upper storey without issues.

Electrical adjustments might include upgrading your service panel to accommodate additional circuits. Each room on your new floor will need power for lighting, heating, and other electrical devices. It's a good idea to plan for more outlets than you think you'll need; future-proofing is key. Also, consider energy-efficient solutions like LED lighting and perhaps even smart home technology, which can all be integrated during the build.

Safety is paramount when dealing with plumbing and electrical systems, so this is definitely not a DIY job. Hiring qualified professionals ensures that all work meets the current regulations and standards, and trust me, you don't want to skimp on this—rewiring or redoing plumbing can be a major hassle and expense if not done correctly the first time.

## Staircase Integration

Integrating a staircase into your existing home isn't just a functional necessity—it's an opportunity to make a statement, or at the very least, blend seamlessly with the aesthetics of your home. The placement of the staircase is critical; it needs to be accessible and logically positioned to flow with the layout of your home, but also constructed in a way that doesn't compromise the structural integrity of the building.

The design of the staircase should consider both aesthetics and space efficiency. Spiral staircases, for example, can be a space-saving solution and add a unique design element, but they might not be suitable for all types of homes or for everyone's needs. A more traditional straight or L-shaped staircase might be preferable for family homes where ease of use is a priority.

Materials for the staircase are another consideration. From solid wood that matches your existing floors to a combination of metal and glass for a modern look, there are numerous options. Each material has its pros and cons in terms of durability, maintenance, and how it complements the rest of your home's interior.

Finally, don't forget about the building regulations related to staircases, which cover everything from the width of the staircase to the height of the handrails. These regulations are designed to ensure safety and accessibility, so make sure that your designs comply.

By tackling these three critical aspects of technical execution—structural supports, plumbing and electrical systems, and staircase integration—you'll ensure that your two-storey extension is not only beautiful but built to last. Remember, meticulous planning and working with experienced professionals are the keys to a successful extension project.

## Living with Construction

Embarking on a two-storey extension is no small feat, and it's not just about the end result. The journey through construction is a critical phase that demands patience, planning, and adaptability. As a homeowner, living through this phase can be challenging, but there are effective strategies to minimise disruptions, ensure safety, and even find temporary solutions to keep your daily life on track.

### Minimising Household Disruption

Firstly, the key to minimising disruption during an extensive construction project like a two-storey extension is all in the preparation. Start by setting up a clear and open line of communication with your builders and architects. Understanding the timeline and phases of construction will give you a heads-up on particularly disruptive activities and allow you to plan around them.

One practical approach is to rearrange your living spaces temporarily. If the construction is concentrated in a specific part of the house, consider relocating your day-to-day activities to quieter, more comfortable areas. For instance, if your kitchen is going to be out of commission, a temporary kitchen setup in another room with essentials like a microwave, a mini-fridge, and a kettle can be a lifesaver.

Sound management is also crucial. Construction inevitably brings noise, which can be one of the most challenging aspects to deal with. Discuss with your contractor about scheduling high-noise tasks at the least disruptive times, and perhaps invest in soundproofing key areas of your home temporarily. Simple solutions like heavy curtains, door seals, and temporary partitions can significantly reduce noise levels.

Lastly, keep the dust down. Dust is an unavoidable byproduct of building work but can be managed effectively. Ensure that your contractor uses dust sheets and that areas are sealed off wherever possible. Regular cleaning – although it might seem like fighting a losing battle – will help prevent the build-up of dust and debris. Air purifiers can also be very beneficial in keeping the air in your home clean, which is especially important if you have young children or family members with allergies.

## Safety During Construction

When it comes to extending your home upwards, the complexity of the work increases, and so does the risk factor. Safety should be your paramount concern, not just for the workers on site but for your household's members as well.

Start by ensuring that your contractor is adhering to all the necessary safety codes and regulations. They should have clear safety protocols in place, which should include securing the construction site at the end of each day to prevent any accidental injuries.

As a homeowner, you should establish safe paths of travel around your property. Make sure that areas of heavy construction are clearly marked and off-limits. If there are days where safety risks are particularly high—during major demolitions or when large materials are being hoisted, for example—it might be wise to plan a day out or a short stay away from home.

If you have children or pets, extra care must be taken to ensure they are kept away from the construction site. Discuss with your builder about erecting secure fencing around the hazardous areas and maintaining a tidy site to avoid any potential accidents.

## Temporary Solutions

Living through a construction project often means being flexible and sometimes creative with temporary solutions to everyday challenges. For example, if your usual laundry facilities are disrupted, it might be time to explore local laundromats or even a laundry service for the duration of the construction. Similarly, if bathroom facilities are affected, consider renting a portable bathroom.

For larger families, or if the disruption is extensive, it might even be worth considering a temporary relocation. Renting a nearby property or staying with relatives could provide a much-needed respite from the daily grind of living on a construction site. While this can add to the project's cost, the reduction in daily stress and the potential for the construction to proceed faster without the household in the way can make this a worthwhile consideration.

Remember, every construction project is unique and presents its own set of challenges and solutions. By planning ahead, maintaining open communication with your contractors, and staying flexible, you can navigate through this disruptive phase with a bit of grace and a lot of patience. Ultimately, these temporary inconveniences will lead to a transformed home that better suits your needs and enhances your lifestyle.

## RECAP AND ACTION ITEMS

Congratulations! You've just navigated through the complexities and opportunities of adding a two-storey extension to your home. By now, you should have a solid understanding of not only the aesthetic and functional advantages but also the technical and practical considerations involved in such a project.

Firstly, let's acknowledge the double advantage a two-storey extension brings. You're not only gaining extra space but doing so without sacrificing additional garden or outdoor areas. This can significantly enhance your property's value and functionality. However, remember the importance of maintaining a balance between your new build's aesthetics and your existing structure to ensure seamless integration.

On the technical front, a two-storey extension requires robust planning, especially regarding structural support, plumbing, and electrical systems. It's crucial to consult with professionals to reinforce the existing foundation and structure to support the additional weight. Additionally, integrating the new plumbing and electrical systems with the existing ones needs careful consideration to ensure efficiency and compliance with building regulations.

Introducing a staircase might seem straightforward, but it's a pivotal element in your extension. It must be functional, complement the overall design, and adhere to safety standards. This is your vertical link between old and new, so make it count.

Living with construction is perhaps the most challenging phase. Minimise disruption by setting up clear boundaries and alternative living arrangements if necessary. Prioritise safety at all times, for both your family and the construction crew. And remember, some temporary solutions during this phase can save a lot of stress.

Now, what should you do next? Here are some actionable steps to take:

**1.Consult Experts:** Engage with architects and structural engineers to discuss your vision and the feasibility of your plans

**2.Planning Permission:** Before proceeding, ensure you have the necessary permissions. This can be a lengthy process, so factor this into your timeline.

**3. Budget Planning:** Set a realistic budget that includes a contingency fund for unforeseen expenses. Remember, investing wisely here can pay dividends in terms of your property's value.

**4. Choose Contractors:** Select experienced contractors who have a track record of working on similar projects. Their expertise will be invaluable.

**5. Communicate:** Keep the lines of communication open with your contractors and designers. Regular updates can help avoid misunderstandings and ensure that the project stays on track.

**6. Prepare for Disruption:** Plan how you'll live during the construction. Whether it's setting up temporary kitchen facilities or even moving out temporarily, plan this in advance.

By taking these steps, you're not just preparing for a successful build but also ensuring that the process is as smooth and stress-free as possible. Here's to making your home bigger and better in every way!

# 5

# TRANSFORMING UNUSED SPACES: GARAGE CONVERSIONS

*"An unused space is a treasure chest waiting to be opened."*
  *~ Martha Stewart*

## Feasibility and Planning

Embarking on a garage conversion is an exhilarating prospect. It's about taking a space that's often cluttered, perhaps even neglected, and transforming it into a vibrant part of your home. Whether you dream of a new home office, a cosy den, or a stylish studio, the journey begins with some solid groundwork in feasibility and planning.

## Assessing Suitability

First things first, you need to determine if your garage is a viable candidate for conversion. Start by evaluating the existing structure. Is the foundation robust enough to support additional weight if you plan on adding walls or heavy appliances? Check the walls and roof for any signs of dampness or deterioration. Issues here could signify a need for significant preliminary repairs before any conversion work can commence.

Consider the space's dimensions too. While a compact garage might be perfect for a snug study room, it may not suit more ambitious plans like a spacious kitchen. Also, think about access points. If the only way in and out of the garage is through a single door, you might need to think about adding additional entries or exits.

Next, examine the surrounding area of your home. Will converting your garage impact the overall aesthetic or functionality of your property? For example, where will you store any items currently housed in the garage? Sometimes, the solution could be as simple as a shed or a storage unit, but this will require additional planning and potentially more expense.

Finally, consider how the conversion will blend with the rest of your house. Consistency in design ensures that the new space doesn't feel disjointed but rather like a seamless extension of your home.

## Design Ideas

Once you've established that your garage can indeed be transformed, it's time to unleash your creativity. Designing your new space can be thrilling, but remember, practicality is just as crucial as aesthetics.

Begin by deciding on the function of the converted space. Your design choices will largely depend on whether you're creating a bedroom, home office, gym, or something else. Each option comes with different considerations for layout, lighting, and storage.

For instance, if you're planning a home office, you might want natural light to reduce eye strain and boost productivity, so consider installing large windows or even skylights. On the other hand, a home cinema room will require different lighting, perhaps focused more on dimmable options to create the right atmosphere.

Think about the existing elements in your garage that could be beneficial. Features like an unusually high ceiling can be turned into a design asset, perhaps by creating a mezzanine level for extra space or storage. Also, remember that certain structural elements might be load-bearing and therefore cannot be removed. Consulting with an architect or structural engineer can help you understand what can and cannot be changed.

Visual coherence between your new room and the rest of your house is also important. Choose materials and finishes that complement the existing interiors. This consideration ensures that the conversion feels integrated rather than tacked on.

## Permit Requirements

Before you get too carried away with planning your dream space, you need to navigate the maze of permit requirements. Regulations can vary significantly by location, so it's essential to check with your local council's planning department to see what rules apply to your project.

Generally, garage conversions typically require planning permission if you are altering the structure of the building or changing its use. For instance, if your garage is attached to your house, the conversion is often considered permitted development (not requiring an application for planning permission), provided you're not enlarging the structure.

However, it's not just about planning permission. Building regulations are another hurdle. These rules ensure that building work meets safety and energy efficiency standards. You'll likely need to submit detailed plans that demonstrate how your conversion will comply with building regulations covering areas such as insulation, ventilation, and fire safety.

Moreover, if you live in a listed building or a conservation area, there are likely to be stricter rules governing changes you can make to your property. In some cases, there might be restrictions on types of materials you can use or specific features that must be preserved.

Navigating these regulations can seem daunting, but don't let this discourage you. Many homeowners go through this process successfully with the right advice and support. Consider consulting with a professional planner or an architect. They can offer invaluable help in ensuring that your plans not only look good on paper but also meet all legal requirements. This step can save you from costly and frustrating setbacks later on.

By carefully considering these three fundamental aspects of feasibility and planning, you're setting a solid foundation for your garage conversion project. Remember, thorough preparation leads to smoother execution and ultimately, a space that enhances your home and your lifestyle.

## The Conversion Process

### Insulation and Damp Proofing

The journey from garage to glorious new room starts with the not-so-glamorous but utterly essential task of insulation and damp proofing. If you're turning your garage into a cosy living space, home office, or a gym, you need to start by creating a comfortable, moisture-free environment. After all, nobody wants to chill or work out in a space that feels like a refrigerator or, worse, a damp cellar!

First up, let's talk about insulation. Most garages are constructed with minimal insulation, as they're originally intended to house cars and store tools, not people. To convert this space into a habitable area, upgrading the insulation is imperative. For walls, consider cavity wall insulation if your garage has double walls. For single, solid walls, internal or external insulation boards can be applied. Remember, adding internal insulation will slightly reduce the room size but it's a trade-off for a warmer, more energy-efficient space.

Next, consider the roof. Heat rises and can escape easily if the roof isn't properly insulated. This can be addressed by installing insulation panels on the underside of the roof. If your garage has a flat roof, you might want to add an extra layer of external insulation when replacing the roofing material.

Floor insulation is often overlooked but equally important. Many garages have concrete floors that are cold and prone to damp. You can opt for a subfloor that includes a damp proof membrane and insulation layer topped with your choice of flooring. This not only helps in keeping the floor warm but also prevents any damp from rising into the room.

Speaking of damp proofing, ensure that there is a robust damp proof course (DPC) in the walls and floor. This is crucial to prevent moisture from seeping into the new living space, which can cause mould and structural issues later on.

## Electrical and Plumbing Needs

Once you've tackled the shell of the room with good insulation and damp proofing, it's time to think about the veins and arteries of your new space: the electrical and plumbing systems.

For electrical installations, you'll likely need more power points than what a typical garage offers. Think about how you plan to use the room and plan your sockets accordingly. Will you need a TV point? How about additional lighting? Perhaps you need internet access or a dedicated space for a home office? Planning this with a qualified electrician is vital, as they can ensure that all electrical work adheres to safety standards and regulations.

If your garage conversion includes adding a kitchenette, bathroom, or even a simple sink, plumbing will come into the picture. This might involve extending your existing plumbing or installing new pipes. Positioning your new facilities close to existing water and waste lines can keep costs down. Consult with a professional plumber to explore the most efficient routes for pipes and to ensure everything complies with local building codes.

Remember, both electrical and plumbing works may require permission from local authorities, so check this during your planning stages to avoid any legal headaches.

## Door and Window Installation

Finally, let's brighten up your new space with some natural light and fresh air by installing new doors and windows. The type and size of windows and doors can drastically affect the feel of your converted garage. Larger windows make the space feel bigger and more welcoming, while well-chosen doors can enhance both the aesthetics and the accessibility.

When choosing windows, think about double-glazing for better thermal and acoustic insulation. For doors, if your garage faces a garden, consider bi-fold or sliding doors to create a seamless indoor-outdoor feel. Not only do these look great, but they also let in plenty of natural light and can be a real feature in your new room.

Installing new doors and windows involves structural work, as openings need to be cut into the existing walls. This is definitely a job for professionals, as it involves considerations around load-bearing walls and maintaining the integrity of the structure. A structural engineer can provide advice and ensure that any modifications comply with safety regulations.

In conclusion, transforming your garage into a usable, comfortable space requires careful attention to insulation, electrical and plumbing systems, and the installation of doors and windows. Each step involves specific challenges and requires professional input, but with the right planning and execution, your new space will enhance your home and lifestyle.

## Making It Your Own

Now that the structure of your garage conversion is solidly in place, it's time to shift gears into the more exciting phase where your personal touch comes into play. This is about more than just a conversion; it's about transformation. Here, you're not just making space; you're crafting a room that feels like a natural part of your home, tailored just for you and your needs. Let's dive into the world of interior finishes and fixtures that will bring your new space to life.

Flooring Choices

Choosing the right flooring for your converted garage can dramatically affect the feel and functionality of your new room. Think about the purpose of your space. Is it a home office, a cosy den, or a vibrant games room? Each requires a different approach to flooring that balances aesthetics with practicality.

**1.Laminate Flooring:** If you're looking for a cost-effective, durable option that's easy to install, laminate flooring might be your best bet. It comes in a variety of finishes, mimicking wood, stone, or even tile, and stands up well to foot traffic. It's also relatively straightforward to maintain, needing only regular sweeping and occasional mopping with a damp cloth.

**2.Engineered Wood:** For a warm, classic look, consider engineered wood. It gives you the beauty of real hardwood but at a more forgiving price point and with better resistance to moisture changes than solid wood, making it particularly suitable for spaces that might still experience slight shifts in temperature and humidity.

**3.Vinyl Flooring:** Modern vinyl flooring is a world away from the patterns of yesteryear, offering remarkable durability and water resistance. It's an excellent choice for utility areas or playrooms where spills and stains are likely. Plus, it's soft underfoot, which can be a bonus in a family-centric space.

**4.Carpet:** Nothing quite matches the warmth and sound insulation provided by a good quality carpet. If your garage is transforming into a snug retreat or a music room, carpet might be perfect. Just remember that maintenance and potential allergen accumulation are considerations worth pondering.

## Heating and Cooling

Achieving a comfortable temperature in your converted garage is crucial for making it feel like part of your home. Here's how you can keep it cosy in winter and cool in the summer:

**1.Radiators:** If your home's central heating system can handle the additional load, extending it into the garage conversion is a seamless way to integrate heating. You'll need to consult with a heating engineer to assess the feasibility of this option.

**2.Underfloor Heating:** For a touch of luxury and an even

distribution of heat, underfloor heating is a great option. It's particularly effective under tile or stone flooring and can free up wall space that radiators otherwise occupy.

**3.Split Air Conditioning and Heating Units:** These offer a dual function, providing heat in the winter and air conditioning in the summer. They are relatively easy to install and don't require ductwork, making them ideal for garage conversions.

**4.Ceiling Fans:** Sometimes, the simplest solutions are the best. A ceiling fan can help circulate air throughout the room, aiding in both heating and cooling by moving warm or cool air around as needed.

## Custom Storage Solutions

Maximising space in your new room means thinking creatively about storage. Custom storage solutions allow you to use every inch of space efficiently, especially in areas that are not standard dimensions.

**1.Built-in Cabinets:** Consider installing built-in cabinets along one wall. They offer a sleek, unobtrusive look and can be designed to fit odd-shaped areas or to house specific items like audio-visual equipment or office supplies.

**2.Shelving Units:** Adjustable shelving units are versatile and can be configured to accommodate books, display items, or bins for toys. They're also relatively easy to install and can be rearranged as your storage needs change.

**3. Hooks and Racks:** Don't overlook the utility of simple solutions like hooks and racks. They're perfect for hanging coats, hats, or even sports equipment, keeping your floor space clear and everything within easy reach.

**4. Overhead Storage:** If your conversion has high ceilings, take advantage of this by installing overhead storage racks. These are ideal for items that you don't use daily but need to keep accessible, such as holiday decorations or seasonal gear.

By focusing on these aspects – flooring, temperature control, and storage – you transform a mere renovated space into a vibrant part of your home that's as functional as it is inviting. Each choice should reflect not just your needs but also your personality, turning the once humble garage into a favourite room in the house where life unfolds and memories are made.

## RECAP AND ACTION ITEMS

You've just navigated through the ins and outs of converting your garage into a functional, appealing space. From assessing the feasibility to adding those finishing touches that truly make it your own, you're now equipped with a blueprint to transform an underutilised area into one of the most valuable spaces in your home.

Let's quickly recap what you've learned so far. First, you evaluated the suitability of your garage for conversion, brainstormed design ideas that align with your needs, and checked out the necessary permits. Then, you tackled the nuts and bolts of the conversion process itself—ensuring proper insulation and damp proofing, addressing electrical and plumbing requirements, and choosing doors and windows that enhance both function and form. Finally, you explored options for flooring, figured out heating and cooling solutions, and planned custom storage to maximise the usability of your new space.

Now, it's time to roll up your sleeves and put this plan into action. Here are the steps you should take next:

**1.Consult Professionals:** Even if you're a DIY enthusiast, consulting with an architect or builder can provide you with invaluable insights and help you avoid costly mistakes.

**2.Secure Permits:** Before you swing that hammer, make sure all your paperwork is in order. Getting the necessary approvals can be a bit of a headache but think of it as the green light to proceed with confidence.

**3.Plan Your Budget:** Keep a close eye on your finances. Remember, good planning can both lower costs and improve outcomes.

**4.Schedule Wisely:** Timing is crucial. Plan your conversion when it least disrupts your daily life, and consider weather conditions, especially if major external work is required.

**5.Choose the Right Materials:** Whether it's insulation materials or flooring, opting for high-quality products will ensure durability and enhance your space's functionality.

**6.Think Long-Term:** Consider how this space will evolve with your needs. Flexible design and adaptable features can accommodate future changes, whether it's a growing family or a new home office requirement.

By following these steps, not only will you add valuable square footage to your home, but you'll also increase its market value—a win-win situation. Remember, every big project is just a series of small steps. Take it one at a time, and soon, you'll be enjoying the fruits of your labour in a beautifully transformed space that was once just a humble garage.

# 6

# REVITALISING YOUR HOME: INTERNAL ALTERATIONS AND RENOVATIONS

*"Your home should tell the story of who you are, and be a collection of what you love."*
  *- Nate Berkus*

## Rethinking Internal Layouts

Let's talk about breathing new life into your home by reimagining its internal layouts. Often, it's not about the space you have but how you use it that counts. Whether you're looking to create a more open, airy environment, want to enhance natural light, or simply need to make better use of the space, rethinking your home's layout can be a game changer.

## Removing or Moving Walls

First off, consider the structure of your home. Walls aren't just physical barriers; they dictate the flow, function, and feel of your spaces. But what if a wall didn't exist where it currently does? Or what if it appeared somewhere else?

Removing or moving walls can dramatically transform your living area, but it's not a decision to be taken lightly or tackled with a sledgehammer on a whim. You'll need to determine whether the wall is load-bearing or not. Load-bearing walls are crucial for your home's structural integrity, supporting the weight above them. If you're considering removing one, it's essential to consult with a structural engineer.

Once you've got the green light, think about how removing or relocating a wall can change the dynamics of your space. Maybe knocking down a wall between your kitchen and living room could create that spacious open-plan living area you've dreamed about. This not only enhances sociability and interaction but can also increase natural light flow throughout the home.

## Open Plan Possibilities

Speaking of open plan, there's a reason why this layout has become a buzzword in contemporary living. An open-plan space can make your home feel larger, lighter, and infinitely more connected. Imagine cooking dinner while chatting with family or guests lounging in the living area — all in one seamless space.

However, open plan living isn't just about demolishing walls and enjoying the new expanse. It's about intelligent design. You need to consider aspects like zoning, which can be achieved with furniture placement, different floor finishes, or even varied ceiling heights to subtly define areas without closing them off.

For instance, a kitchen island can act as a perfect divider that also serves as a functional prep and socialising spot. Rugs and lighting can anchor a living area within a larger space, creating a cosy enclave.

## Enhancing Natural Light

The third transformative power play in your layout revamping strategy is optimising natural light. Natural light not only makes a space feel more inviting and larger but also boosts your mood and energy levels.

Start by assessing the current natural light sources in your home. Are there areas that feel gloomy or disconnected from the outdoors? Sometimes, the solution can be as simple as changing the type or size of window treatments. Opting for sheer blinds or removing heavy drapes can invite more light into the room.

Consider also the possibility of introducing new windows or

even skylights in darker areas of your home. Skylights are particularly effective for bringing light into central parts of a house that may not have direct access to exterior walls.

Another aspect to consider is the orientation of your rooms. Rooms used most during the day should ideally get plenty of natural light. If this isn't the case, think about how you might switch up the uses of your rooms to align with the sun's path.

Mirror placements can also amplify light. By positioning mirrors directly opposite windows, you can double the amount of sunlight entering a room, making it feel brighter and more open.

By rethinking your internal layouts through these strategies — removing or moving walls, exploring open plan possibilities, and enhancing natural light — you can significantly change how your home looks and feels. These alterations not only improve the aesthetics and functionality of your space but can also add to its value, making it a smart move for any homeowner looking to invest in their property. Remember, the goal is to create a home that feels both welcoming and uniquely yours, adapting not just to your aesthetic tastes but also to your lifestyle needs.

## Modernising Utilities

Upgrading heating systems, integrating smart home technology, and enhancing water efficiency are not just buzzwords— they are essential components in modernising the utilities in your home. These improvements not only make your home more comfortable and convenient but can also lead to significant savings on energy bills and contribute to a more sustainable planet. Let's dive into how you can bring your home into the 21st century, starting with your heating system.

## Upgrading Heating Systems

One of the most impactful changes you can make in your home is upgrading your heating system. Traditional systems often use more energy than necessary and can leave cold spots in rooms—something you definitely want to avoid during chilly winters. If you're still relying on an old boiler and radiator setup, it might be time for a change.

Consider installing a condensing boiler. These are not only more energy-efficient but they also convert more gas into heat, reducing wastage and saving you money on gas bills. Look for models with an "A" energy efficiency rating to ensure maximum efficiency.

Underfloor heating is another fantastic option, especially if you're already planning to change your floors. It distributes heat more evenly than traditional radiators, and because it operates at a lower temperature while still warming a room effectively, it can reduce your energy consumption. Plus, it frees up wall space, giving you more freedom in your interior design choices.

Think also about controls and thermostats. Smart thermostats allow you to control your home's temperature remotely via your smartphone. This means you can turn the heating on or off or adjust the temperature even when you're not at home, ensuring that you're always coming back to a warm house without wasting energy heating it when it's empty.

## Smart Home Technology

Incorporating smart home technology goes beyond just installing a smart thermostat. This technology can enhance the functionality, security, and efficiency of your home in myriad ways.

Let's start with lighting. Smart lighting systems allow you to control the lights in your home remotely or via schedules you set according to your daily routines. You can adjust brightness, switch lights on or off, and even change colours if you opt for RGB LED lights. These adjustments not only cater to your mood but also help in reducing your electrical consumption by ensuring lights aren't left on unnecessarily.

Security is another major aspect of smart home technology. Smart locks and security systems provide you with real-time alerts and remote access, offering peace of mind whether you're at home or away. Cameras, motion detectors, and entry sensors make it easier to keep an eye on your property.

Lastly, consider smart appliances. From fridges that remind

you when you're out of milk to ovens that you can preheat on your way home from work, these appliances offer a level of convenience and efficiency that traditional models can't match. They can also provide insights into your usage patterns, helping you to make adjustments that save energy and reduce costs.

## Water Efficiency

Water efficiency is often overlooked in discussions about utility modernisation, but it's crucial for both environmental sustainability and reducing your water bills. A few changes in fixtures and habits can make a substantial difference.

Start with the basics: taps and showerheads. Installing aerated or low-flow models can reduce water usage dramatically without sacrificing water pressure. These fixtures use air to bulk up the flow, meaning less water is needed to achieve the same effect.

Consider the heart of water usage in many homes: the bathroom. Low-flush and dual-flush toilets can save a significant amount of water compared to traditional models. They use just enough water to flush effectively, which can cut your household water use by up to 30%.

Don't forget about outside water use. Rainwater harvesting systems collect rainwater from your roof that can be used for watering the garden, washing cars, or even for flushing toilets and washing clothes. These systems can reduce your dependence on mains water and lower your water bill.

In conclusion, when you decide to modernise the utilities in your home, you're not just updating your space; you're investing in your home's future. These changes can increase your comfort, reduce your bills, and significantly decrease your environmental footprint. Take the time to consider which options best suit your needs and make a plan to implement them. With these upgrades, your home will not just be a place to live—it will be a more efficient, smarter living environment.

## Decor and Aesthetics

When it comes to revitalising your home, never underestimate the power of decor and aesthetics. This isn't just about splashing a new coat of paint on the walls or tossing a new rug on the floor; it's about creating a cohesive look that reflects your personal style and enhances your living space. Let's break down the essentials: colour schemes, furniture selection, and art and accessories.

### Colour Schemes

Choosing the right colour scheme is pivotal—it sets the mood for your entire home. Think about what kind of atmosphere you want to create. Are you looking for a calm and relaxing space, or something vibrant and energising? Colours aren't just beauty;

they're also psychology. Soft blues and greens evoke serenity, making them perfect for bedrooms or bathrooms, while bold reds and oranges can inject vitality into a kitchen or dining area.

Don't just think about the walls. Consider how the colours of your furniture, flooring, and even light fixtures will interact. If you're going for a minimalist look, you might opt for a monochromatic scheme using varying shades of the same colour. For those a bit more adventurous, try a complementary scheme with colours opposite each other on the colour wheel, like blue and orange. This can add a dynamic element to your space.

A practical tip is to use testers—those little pots of paint you can buy to test colours on your walls. Observe how different colours look throughout the day as natural light changes. This can greatly influence your final choice, ensuring you won't have any regrets once the entire room is done.

## Furniture Selection

Selecting the right furniture is not just about style; it's about function and form working harmoniously in your space. Start by assessing your needs. What activities take place in each room? Does your living room double as a workspace? If so, you might consider a sleek, comfortable sofa that's good for both relaxing and sitting up to work.

The size of your furniture is also crucial. In a smaller room, oversized furniture can make the space feel cramped and vice versa. Try using scaled pieces of paper placed on the floor to help visualise how much space different items will occupy before you commit to buying them.

Material matters, too. Natural materials like wood and leather not only look classy but are generally more durable. However, if you have pets or young children, you might consider more forgiving and easy-to-clean materials like microfiber.

And remember, furniture placement can significantly affect the feel of a room. Even the most beautiful pieces won't shine if they disrupt the flow of the space. Ensure there's enough room to move around comfortably, and consider the sight lines from various points in the room. This can make your space not just beautiful, but functional.

## Art and Accessories

Finally, let's talk about the cherries on top: art and accessories. These are what give your home its character and uniqueness, so this is where you can really express yourself.

Start with art. What resonates with you? Art isn't always a grandiose, framed piece. It can be anything from a traditional oil painting to modern digital prints or even a tapestry. When hanging art, consider the eye level; the centre of the piece should be at eye level for an average person. Also, think about the scale; a small painting on a large wall can look lost, so consider larger pieces or a group of smaller pieces for bigger walls.

Next, accessories. These range from cushions and throws to vases and books. They are an excellent way to introduce texture and layer into your space. Mix materials like metal, glass, ceramics, and fabrics for a curated look. For instance, a velvet throw can add a touch of luxury to a leather sofa, while a rough, wooden coffee table can bring a sense of ruggedness to an otherwise sleek living room.

When accessorising, think in vignettes or small groupings. These can be more visually appealing than scattering single items around. However, beware of clutter. It's easy to go overboard, so always step back and assess whether each item really needs to be there.

By carefully selecting your colour schemes, furniture, and accessories, you can transform your home into a space that not only looks impressive but feels uniquely yours. Remember, the goal of redecorating is to create a space where you feel comfortable and relaxed, surrounded by things that inspire and uplift you. Whether you're embarking on a major overhaul or just making a few small changes, these elements are crucial in achieving the aesthetic that best suits your lifestyle and taste.

## RECAP AND ACTION ITEMS

Congratulations on navigating through the essential strategies for revitalising your home through internal alterations and renovations. By now, you've gathered a wealth of ideas to not only enhance the functionality of your living space but to also elevate its overall aesthetic appeal.

Firstly, rethinking your internal layouts has likely sparked exciting ideas about removing or moving walls to create a more fluid and adaptable environment. Embracing open plan possibilities may have opened your eyes to a home that fosters both communication and togetherness. Moreover, introducing strategies to enhance natural light has the potential to transform your living spaces into bright, energy-efficient areas.

Moving on to modernising utilities, you've explored upgrading heating systems, integrating smart home technology, and improving water efficiency. These advancements are not just about following trends; they are about making smart choices that will benefit your lifestyle, budget, and the environment in the long run.

Lastly, we delved into decor and aesthetics. Choosing the right colour schemes, selecting furniture that complements your living space, and accessorising with art can personalise and style your home, making it truly yours.

Now, for the action items. Here's what you can do next:

**1.Assess and Plan:** Evaluate the current layout and utilities of your home. Identify which walls could be removed or moved, and decide if an open plan is suitable for your lifestyle. Assess your current heating and water systems to pinpoint which areas need upgrades.

**2. Consult the Experts:** For structural changes, such as removing walls, and major utility upgrades, it's wise to consult with professionals. Architects, interior designers, and structural engineers can provide valuable insights and help avoid costly mistakes.

**3. Explore Technology Options:** Research the latest in smart home technology. Start small with smart thermostats or lighting systems as these can offer both convenience and cost savings. Gradually integrate more as you see fit.

**4. Visualise Your Aesthetic:** Create a mood board that includes potential colour schemes, furniture pieces, and accessories. This visual guide will help you maintain a cohesive style throughout your renovation process.

**5. Budget and Timeline:** Set a realistic budget and timeline for your renovation projects. Consider tackling one room at a time or one major change at a time to keep things manageable.

**6. Implement in Phases:** Start with the changes that will have the most immediate impact on your lifestyle and well-being, such as improving natural light or upgrading the heating system.

**7. Reflect on Your Space:** As you make these changes, take time to reflect on how each alteration makes you feel in your home. Adjust your plans as needed to ensure your home meets your evolving needs.

By breaking these projects down into actionable steps, you can systematically transform your house into a home that not only looks spectacular but also enhances your day-to-day living. Remember, revitalising your home is a journey, not a race. Take it one step at a time and enjoy the process of creating a space that truly reflects who you are.

# 7

# CHOOSING THE RIGHT CONTRACTOR

*"The bitterness of poor quality remains long after the sweetness of low price is forgotten."*
  *– Benjamin Franklin*

## The Importance of Expertise

When you're setting out to make significant improvements to your home, whether it's extending your kitchen, converting an attic into a liveable space, or renovating a dated bathroom, choosing the right contractor can feel as critical as the project itself. The expertise of the contractor is the bedrock on which the success of your project will be built. Let's delve into what makes expertise so vital, covering key areas such as credentials and experience, references and portfolios, and specialisations.

## Credentials and Experience

Imagine you're a chef about to create a banquet. Would you choose someone who's only ever fried an egg to be your sous chef? Unlikely. This is the mindset to adopt when assessing the credentials and experience of a contractor. Credentials act as a baseline guarantee that the contractor has the training and knowledge to handle the job. In the UK, reputable contractors often hold accreditations from recognised bodies such as the Federation of Master Builders (FMB) or the National Federation of Builders (NFB). These aren't just fancy titles; they signify a commitment to maintaining certain standards in the construction industry.

Experience, however, tells you more about the breadth and depth of their capabilities. A contractor like Prime Joinery, with years of successful projects under their belt, brings a reassurance that can't be matched by newcomers. It's not just about longevity but the relevance of their experience to your specific project. If you're looking at extending your property, for instance, seeing that Prime Joinery has successfully managed multiple extensions gives you a concrete sense of their capability.

## References and Portfolios

Moving onto references and portfolios – think of these as the trailer to the movie. They offer you sneak peeks into the actual workings and outcomes of past projects. A robust portfolio showcases not just the final look but the range and diversity of projects undertaken. It's one thing to claim expertise in renovations, but another to display transformative before-and-after pictures of a variety of properties, from Victorian terraces to modern flats.

References, on the other hand, add another layer of credibility. Speaking to previous clients of Prime Joinery can offer insights that a portfolio can't. Was the contractor reliable? Did they communicate effectively? How did they handle the unexpected? These testimonials build a picture of the working relationship you might expect and underline the trust previous homeowners have placed in their hands.

## Specialisations

Finally, let's talk about specialisations. Every home improvement project has its peculiarities. Some might be straightforward, requiring standard know-how, while others might involve complex structural changes demanding specialised skills. This is where understanding a contractor's specialisations becomes crucial.

For example, if you're considering a green home improvement, such as installing solar panels or upgrading to sustainable building materials, would it not be wise to engage a contractor who specialises in eco-friendly constructions? Prime Joinery, known for their bespoke joinery work, exemplifies a specialist skill set that can significantly enhance projects involving unique woodwork or custom-made fittings. Their expertise in this niche area ensures that not only will the functional aspects of your renovation be handled but also that aesthetic and bespoke details are crafted to a high standard.

Choosing a contractor with the right specialisations means that no aspect of your vision is left to chance. Whether it's a need for intricate detail in joinery or expertise in period property renovations, a specialised contractor brings a depth of knowledge and an assurance that they can navigate the specific challenges of your project.

Navigating through the maze of contractor choices can be daunting. However, understanding the importance of expertise—encompassed by their credentials and experience, the quality of their references and portfolios, and the relevance of their specialisations—will guide you to make a decision that aligns with your vision for your home. Remember, the right contractor is not just a builder; they are a partner in bringing your dream home to life

## Communication and Contracts

When you're diving into the world of home improvements, the clarity of communication and the solidity of contracts can't be overstated. These are not just formalities; they're your safety nets and blueprints for success. Let's break it down into digestible parts, so you can navigate this crucial aspect with the finesse of a seasoned pro.

## Clear Agreements

First things first, the cornerstone of any successful homeowner-contractor relationship lies in clear agreements. Imagine you're planning a major renovation with Prime Joinery, known for their meticulous craftsmanship in joinery and beyond. You wouldn't want to start off with just a handshake or verbal agreement, right? Here's where the magic of a well-drafted contract comes into play.

A contract should be comprehensive—it should outline every detail from the scope of work and materials used, to timelines and payment schedules. It's not just about protecting yourself legally; it's about having a clear roadmap of the project. For instance, if you're adding a sleek new extension to your home, you'd want everything specified, from the type of wood used for the cabinetry to the finish on the handles.

Make sure that every aspect of the project is covered. If Prime Joinery suggests a specific type of wood that adjusts well to your local climate, get that detailed in the contract. It's these nuances that can make or break the functional and aesthetic aspects of your renovation.

## Ongoing Dialogue

Now, onto the lifeline of any project - ongoing dialogue. Think of your relationship with your contractor as a partnership rather than a transaction. Regular communication is key to ensuring this partnership thrives. Set up regular check-ins with your contractor, be it weekly or bi-weekly, to discuss progress, any challenges that have surfaced, and adjustments needed.

With a contractor like Prime Joinery, renowned for their client-focused approach, these discussions can be incredibly fruitful. They're not just updating you; they're engaging with you to share insights, offer solutions, and sometimes, to bring up new ideas that could elevate your project. This open line of communication ensures that you are always in the loop and confident about where the project is heading.

Remember, effective communication should be two-way. It's equally important for you to provide feedback or voice concerns. If, say, the initial wood choice for your kitchen cabinets is not turning out as expected, these regular dialogues provide the perfect opportunity to discuss alternatives or tweaks.

## Handling Disputes

No matter how well you plan, disputes can arise. Maybe it's a delay in the delivery of materials or a misunderstanding about a particular design element; how these disputes are handled can significantly affect your project's timeline and outcome.

The key here is to have a dispute resolution clause in your contract. This sets the protocol for handling disagreements before they escalate into major issues. For instance, Prime Joinery might have a procedure in place where any disputes are first handled internally through a structured mediation process. This often involves revisiting the contract, discussing the points of contention, and coming to a mutual agreement on how to move forward.

It's also wise to keep records of all communications and decisions made throughout the project. This can be invaluable in resolving any disputes as it provides a clear historical context of who said what and when.

In conclusion, navigating the world of contractor relationships through clear agreements, ongoing dialogue, and effective dispute resolution can transform a potentially stressful renovation into a manageable, even enjoyable project. With a contractor like Prime Joinery, you're not just hiring a service; you're partnering with professionals who are invested in making your home as beautiful and functional as you envision it. So, set the foundation right with solid communication and contracts, and watch your home transform seamlessly.

## Monitoring Progress

When you're waist-deep in a home renovation or extension project, staying on top of progress is crucial. It's not just about ensuring that work is completed on time; it's also about making sure it meets your expectations for quality and detail. Let's dive into how you can effectively monitor the progress of your home improvement project, especially when working with skilled outfits like Prime Joinery.

### Regular Updates

The first step to effectively monitoring your project is to establish a routine for regular updates. This is your project's pulse check. It's essential to agree on how often you will receive progress reports from your contractor. Weekly? Bi-weekly? The frequency might depend on the scope and duration of the project, but the key is consistency.

With a contractor like Prime Joinery, you might find that they are proactive with these updates. They understand that you're not just investing money; you're also investing your trust and vision in their hands. Regular updates should be detailed and should ideally include what has been completed, any modifications from the original plan, and what is scheduled next. Photographs and videos can be incredibly helpful here, giving you a clear visual confirmation of what's being reported.

These updates are also a good time to verify timelines. Check if the project is on track to meet the deadlines or if there are any delays to be expected. If your contractor isn't forthcoming with regular updates, don't hesitate to initiate them yourself. Remember, it's your home, and staying informed puts you in the driver's seat.

## Quality Checks

The backbone of any renovation or construction project is the quality of the work done. This is where the rubber meets the road. Regular quality checks are essential to ensure that the work completed meets the high standards you expect and adheres to all relevant regulations and codes.

With a seasoned contractor like Prime Joinery, quality checks are often ingrained in their process. However, it's advisable for you as the homeowner to be involved or even to insist on periodic, independent inspections. These can be conducted by a third-party professional who can assess the craftsmanship and materials used. This step is not about mistrusting your contractor but ensuring accountability.

During these checks, look at the fine details. Are the finishes as per the sample you approved? Are the installations aligned and secure? Small discrepancies can lead to bigger issues later, so it's crucial to catch them early. This phase is also the time to address any concerns you have about the work done. Effective communication during these checks can prevent a lot of headaches as the project moves forward.

## Adjustments and Approvals

As much as everyone hopes for a project to go exactly to plan, the reality is often different. Adjustments might be necessary, whether due to unforeseen structural issues, delays in material supply, or simply because you've changed your mind about something. This is a normal part of home improvement projects, and managing these adjustments smoothly can significantly impact the success of your project.

When you work with Prime Joinery, you'll find that they are typically flexible and responsive to changes. However, every adjustment should be documented and approved by both parties. This isn't just bureaucracy; it's protection for both you and the contractor. It ensures everyone is on the same page and that you're not faced with unexpected changes or charges later on.

Approvals are just as crucial. Each major phase of the project should be signed off by you before moving on to the next. This sign-off can be formal, with a physical or digital document, or it could be a verbal confirmation with a follow-up email for records. This step reaffirms your satisfaction with the work and can be critical when making final payments.

Monitoring the progress of your home improvement effectively ensures that the project remains aligned with your vision and is executed to your satisfaction. Establishing a clear, structured way to receive updates, conduct quality checks, and manage adjustments keeps you firmly in control. Remember, a reputable contractor like Prime Joinery will support these efforts because, ultimately, their goal is to deliver a result that you love. So, stay engaged, insist on transparency, and watch as your home transforms.

## RECAP AND ACTION ITEMS

Choosing the right contractor isn't just a box-ticking exercise—it's a critical step in transforming your house into your dream home. By understanding the importance of expertise, the nuances of communication and contracts, and the essentials of monitoring progress, you're well on your way to a successful home improvement project.

Let's break it down into actionable steps to ensure you harness the full potential of this knowledge.

**1. Evaluate Expertise:** Start by verifying credentials and experience. Don't shy away from asking for and actually calling references, and insist on viewing portfolios. A contractor like Prime Joinery, known for its robust portfolio and glowing testimonials, sets a high standard you should look for.

**2. Document Everything:** When you've chosen your contractor, nail down the specifics in a clear, comprehensive contract. Detail every aspect of the project from timelines to materials, and costs to warranties. This clarity will save you countless headaches.

**3. Establish Communication Rhythms:** Set up regular check-ins from the outset. These can be weekly or bi-weekly meetings where you discuss progress, address any concerns, and adjust plans as necessary. Remember, effective dialogue can make or break a project.

**4. Quality Control:** Schedule regular on-site visits, preferably at milestones agreed upon in your contract. Use these visits to conduct quality checks and ensure the project aligns with your expectations. If adjustments are necessary, don't hesitate to speak up. Your satisfaction is paramount.

**5. Stay Flexible but Firm:** While flexibility is important in handling unexpected changes or challenges, maintaining your project's core goals and standards is equally crucial. Approve adjustments only when they align with your overall vision and budget.

**6. Final Walk-through and Approval:** Before signing off on the project, conduct a thorough final inspection alongside your contractor. This is your opportunity to ensure that every detail meets your standards and that any final tweaks are made before the final handshake.

By following these steps, you'll be better equipped to manage your home renovation project effectively. With a trusted partner like Prime Joinery, you can be confident in both the journey and the outcome. Remember, the right contractor doesn't just help build a structure but helps realise your vision of a perfect home.

# 8

# BUDGETING FOR YOUR PROJECT

*"A budget tells us what we can't afford, but it doesn't keep us from buying it."*
  *- William Feather*

## Cost Estimation Basics

Embarking on a home improvement project is a thrilling venture. It's like setting off on a cross-country road trip without a clear map; excitement is in the air, but so is the potential for unexpected detours and hidden roadblocks. To make your journey as smooth as possible, you need to master the art of cost estimation. This isn't just about figuring out how much everything will cost upfront; it's about understanding the full financial landscape of your project. Let's dive into the fundamentals, shall we?

## Initial Estimates

First things first, you need to get a grip on your initial estimates. This is your starting line, the baseline from which all financial decisions will spring. Think of it as setting up your chessboard before the game begins; you need to position your pieces (or pennies) wisely.

Start by breaking down your project into bite-sized pieces. Are you planning an extension, a conversion, or perhaps a full-scale renovation? Each segment of your project will have its own set of costs, from materials to labour. Your job is to list these out as comprehensively as possible. Don't just scribble down numbers; do your homework. Talk to contractors, get quotes, and maybe even consult with an architect. Remember, the more detailed your initial estimate, the better prepared you'll be.

But here's a pro tip: always add a buffer. Most homeowners will stick a neat 10% on top of their estimates for good measure, but why not consider pushing that to 15% or even 20%? It might sound a bit much now, but when the unexpected knocks on your door, you'll be glad you had that extra cushion.

## Hidden Costs

Speaking of the unexpected, let's chat about hidden costs. These are the ninjas of the cost estimation world; they're stealthy, and you often don't see them coming until it's too late. Hidden costs can include anything from unforeseen structural issues (like discovering your entire plumbing system needs replacing) to legal fees that weren't obvious at the outset.

One classic hidden cost is 'scope creep' - that's when your project slowly expands beyond its original boundaries. Maybe you decide halfway through that you want underfloor heating, or perhaps those kitchen fittings you chose originally just won't cut it anymore. These changes can inflate your budget quicker than a balloon on a windy day.

To combat these sneaky expenses, you need vigilance and flexibility. Keep a close eye on your project as it progresses, and hold regular check-ins with your contractors to ensure everything is staying on track. Additionally, set aside a contingency fund specifically for these hidden costs. Around 20% of your total budget should go into this pot, giving you a financial parachute should you need to jump out of a cost overrun plane.

## Value Engineering

Now, onto a brighter subject: value engineering. This isn't about cutting costs willy-nilly; it's about spending smarter, not harder. Value engineering is the art of enhancing your project's function or quality while reducing costs. It's finding the sweet spot between what you need and what you can afford without compromising on aesthetics or functionality.

Here's how you can apply value engineering to your project:

start by re-evaluating your design and materials. Ask yourself if there are more cost-effective alternatives that won't detract from the end result. For instance, could you opt for a less expensive type of flooring that still looks superb and wears well? Could you simplify a complex design to save on construction costs without losing the impact?

Also, consider the long-term value of your choices. It might be worth investing a bit more upfront for energy-efficient windows that will save you money on heating bills down the road. Or perhaps installing solar panels could be a smart move, offering you energy savings and potential government incentives.

In essence, value engineering is about making informed decisions that balance cost with quality. By taking this approach, you can not only keep your project within budget but also enhance the overall value of your home, making it a smarter, more functional, and more enjoyable place to live.

As you navigate through these cost estimation basics, remember that preparation is your best friend. The more you understand and plan for both the seen and unseen costs, the smoother your home improvement journey will be. So, take these insights, apply them with wisdom, and transform your home into the haven you've always dreamed it could be.

# Financing Options

When you're ready to turn your house into your dream home, figuring out how to finance the renovation is as crucial as choosing the right tiles for your bathroom. Let's dive into the options available that can help transform your blueprint dreams into brick-and-mortar reality without breaking the bank.

Loans and Credits

One of the most straightforward paths to funding your home improvement project is through loans and credits. This route offers several options, each with its own set of advantages and considerations.

**\*Personal Loans:\*** A personal loan can be a great option if you have a good credit score and require funds quickly. Banks, credit unions, and online lenders offer personal loans that are often unsecured, meaning they don't require your home as collateral. The amount you can borrow varies, typically up to £25,000 or £35,000, with repayment terms ranging from one to seven years. The interest rates might be higher than secured loans, but the application process is usually simpler and faster.

**\*Secured Home Improvement Loans:\*** If you need to borrow a larger amount, consider a secured home improvement loan. These are linked to your property as collateral, which often results in lower interest rates compared to unsecured loans.

Keep in mind, however, that your property is at risk if you fail to make payments. Loan terms can extend up to10-20 years, depending on the amount borrowed and your lender.

**Credit Cards:** For smaller projects or short-term financing, credit cards can be useful, especially those offering0% interest on purchases for an introductory period. This can be a smart move if you can pay off the balance before the standard interest rate kicks in. It's also a handy way to gain rewards or cashback if your credit card offers these perks.

When considering loans and credits, it's vital to shop around and compare the APR (Annual Percentage Rate), terms, and any hidden fees. Use online comparison tools to find the best deals tailored to your financial situation.

## Government Grants

Believe it or not, you might find that you don't always have to shoulder the financial load alone. The UK government and various local councils sometimes provide grants to help homeowners improve their properties, especially for energy-saving upgrades and essential repairs.

**Green Homes Grant:** This scheme allows homeowners and residential landlords to apply for vouchers towards the cost of installing energy-efficient improvements to their homes. You could get funding for up to two-thirds of the cost of the eligible improvements, up to £5,000, or even more for low-income households.

**Disabled Facilities Grant:** If you need to modify your home due to a disability, this grant can help towards the costs of making it more accessible. This might include widening doors, installing ramps, or improving access to rooms and facilities. The amount you can get depends on your household income and savings, with a maximum of £30,000 in England.

Check with your local council or the Energy Saving Trust website to find out what grants might be available in your area. These grants not only help with financing but also ensure that your home improvements are environmentally conscious or enhance your living conditions significantly.

## Private Financing

Sometimes, traditional lending options and grants might not cover all your needs, or perhaps you're looking for a more flexible funding solution. This is where private financing comes into play, offering a range of possibilities that might suit your specific circumstances.

**Home Equity Line of Credit (HELOC):** This type of credit works like a credit card but with your home as collateral. You're approved for a certain amount and can draw from it as needed, making it ideal for ongoing or phased projects. Interest is only paid on the amount you use, and the interest rates are generally more favourable than those on personal loans.

**\*Peer-to-Peer Lending:\*** Platforms like Funding Circle or Zopa allow you to borrow money directly from investors instead of going through a traditional financial institution. The rates can be competitive, especially if you have a good credit rating, and the application process is often straightforward and digital.

**\*Bridge Financing:\*** If you're in the process of selling your old home while renovating your new one, bridge financing might be a useful option. It provides a short-term loan to cover the gap between buying your new home and selling your old one. It's a bit riskier and more expensive than other types of loans, so it's typically used as a last resort.

Whichever financing route you choose, ensure it aligns with your financial health and long-term goals. Always read the fine print, understand the repayment terms, and consider how the monthly payments will fit into your budget. Remember, well-planned financing can make the difference between a stressful renovation and an enjoyable transformation of your living space.

## Keeping on Track

### Budget Management

When you're steering the ship of a home improvement project, consider yourself as much a budget manager as a homeowner. It's not just about choosing the right tiles or the perfect shade of paint; it's about keeping a tight rein on your finances to ensure your project doesn't end up costing you an arm and a leg. Start by setting up a clear, itemised budget. List out every foreseeable expense, from materials and labour to permits and pizzas for the friends who help you paint.

Once your budget is set, it's essential to track every penny spent. Tools like spreadsheets or budgeting apps can be your best friends here, allowing you to keep a real-time overview of your expenses versus your initial estimates. Be disciplined about updating your costs as soon as they occur. This habit will help you spot any financial deviation early and adjust before it spirals.

Another smart move is to set aside a contingency fund, ideally around 10-20% of your total budget. This isn't an invitation to splurge but a safety net for those unforeseen issues that might otherwise force you to compromise on quality or design.

Regularly review your budget as the project progresses. This might seem a bit tedious, but it's crucial. Weekly check-ins are a good rhythm for most projects. Use this time to compare your spending against the plan and forecast the next phase of expenses. If you find yourself consistently underspending, it's a chance to re-evaluate and possibly enhance aspects of the project. Conversely, if you're overspending, it's time to tighten the belt, re-prioritise, or lean on your contingency fund if necessary.

## Avoiding Overspends

Overspending can be the bane of home improvements. The good news? With a proactive approach, it's largely avoidable. First, be crystal clear about your priorities. Know where you want to splurge and where you're prepared to save. For instance, investing in high-quality kitchen fittings might be non-negotiable, but perhaps you could opt for a less expensive option for the guest bathroom tiles.

When it comes to purchasing materials, compare prices and don't shy away from negotiating discounts, especially for large orders. Establish good relationships with suppliers – they might tip you off on upcoming sales or bulk discount opportunities. Also, consider the timing of your purchases. Buying off-season can often save you a pretty penny, especially on items like garden equipment and outdoor furniture.

Another common pitfall is the "while we're at it" syndrome. This happens when you start making incremental additions to the project ("Since we're redoing the kitchen, why not knock down this wall and make an open plan?"). While it's tempting to expand your project scope, each addition needs to be carefully considered against your budget. Always go back to your financial plan and assess the impact of any new ideas before giving them the green light.

DIY can also be a great way to control costs, provided you realistically assess your skills and the time commitment needed. Tackling painting, tiling, or even some basic carpentry can reduce labour costs significantly. However, know when to call in the professionals. Complex electrical work, plumbing, or structural changes not only require expert skills but are also often legally bound to be carried out by licensed tradespeople.

## Dealing with Unexpected Costs

No matter how meticulously you plan, unexpected costs in home improvement projects are as predictable as rain in London. Maybe you discover dampness while replacing the bathroom floor, or perhaps structural issues come to light during a loft conversion. Such surprises can be disheartening and potentially expensive, but they don't have to derail your project.

First, don't panic. Revisit your budget and see where adjustments can be made. Can non-essential elements be deferred? Is there wiggle room in your contingency fund to cover the extra expense? If the answer is no, it's time to think creatively about alternative solutions that won't blow your budget. For example, if the cost of materials has soared unexpectedly, could you substitute them for something more economical yet still aesthetically pleasing?

Communication with your contractors is also key. Ensure they understand the importance of sticking to the budget and encourage them to come to you with any financial concerns as soon as they arise, rather than when the bill is due. Sometimes, a contractor can suggest a more cost-effective way of achieving the same result.

Lastly, keep documentation of all unexpected expenses. Not only does this help with your current budget management, but it also provides a valuable reference for any future projects. Knowing what went over budget and why can help you plan more accurately next time, turning unforeseen headaches into valuable learning experiences.

By mastering these aspects of budget management, avoiding unnecessary overspends, and tactically handling unexpected costs, you can keep your project on track financially without compromising on your vision. Remember, effective financial oversight is not about scrimping at every corner; it's about making informed decisions that align with your priorities and ensuring your home improvement journey is as stress-free as possible.

## RECAP AND ACTION ITEMS

Navigating the financial aspects of home improvement can be as intricate as redesigning a complex blueprint. You now have a solid foundation in cost estimation basics, financing options, and strategies to keep your project on budget. Let's cement that knowledge with clear, actionable steps you can take to ensure your home improvement dreams don't turn into financial nightmares.

Firstly, refer back to the initial estimates you've drafted. These are your blueprint for financial planning. Now that you understand the potential for hidden costs and the value of engineering your project efficiently, revisit these estimates. Adjust them with a critical eye—where can you possibly cut costs without cutting corners? This is your first action step: refine your budget with precision and foresight.

Next, financing your project might seem daunting, but you have options. Whether it's loans, government grants, or private financing, your task is to research which avenue best suits your financial situation. Contact your local bank, explore government websites, or maybe schedule a meeting with a financial advisor. Your action step here is to gather all necessary information and apply for the appropriate financial support to kickstart your project.

Lastly, keeping on track is crucial. Set up a system for budget management—this could be as simple as a spreadsheet or a dedicated software. Regularly monitor your expenses and adjust as necessary. Remember, the goal is to avoid overspends and effectively manage unexpected costs. Make it a habit to review your budget weekly. If anything deviates from your plan, you'll be prepared to take swift action.

By following these steps, you'll not only manage your home improvement project more effectively but also potentially increase the value of your property and enhance your living environment. Remember, a well-planned project is a well-executed project. Take control, stay informed, and push forward with confidence. Your ideal home is within reach, and now you have the tools to build it wisely.

# 9

# MANAGING THE BUILD

*"Quality is never an accident; it is always the result of intelligent effort."*
  – *John Ruskin*

## Scheduling and Timelines

Embarking on a home improvement project can be as thrilling as it is daunting. Whether you're extending your kitchen, converting an attic into a cosy nook, or giving your entire home a facelift, the success of your project hinges significantly on how well you manage time. Let's break down how you can master the art of scheduling and timelines, ensuring your project runs as smoothly as your morning espresso.

## Creating a Realistic Timeline

First and foremost, setting a realistic timeline for your project is crucial. I know, the excitement is palpable and you want everything done yesterday. But, let's channel that enthusiasm into planning. Every significant achievement needs a solid foundation, and in the realm of home improvements, that foundation is a well-crafted timeline.

Start by understanding the scope of your project. Sit down with your contractor or architect and discuss every phase of the work. You need to know what will happen and when it will happen. This includes everything from initial demolitions to the final touches of paint. It's not just about setting start and end dates; you need to consider the sequence of tasks, how long each task will take, and the dependencies between tasks. For instance, you can't start painting if the plastering isn't dry.

Consult with professionals to get accurate estimates on how long each part of the project will take. Remember, precision here is key. It's also wise to discuss potential roadblocks that could cause delays. Maybe there are certain times of the year when weather could impede outdoor work, or perhaps you're renovating in an area where deliveries can be tricky.

Once you have all the details, draft a timeline using a Gantt chart or a similar project management tool. These tools allow you to visualise the project from start to finish, providing a clear picture of how different tasks overlap and link with each other. This visual approach can help you spot potential problems before they arise.

## Prioritising Tasks

With your timeline set, it's time to prioritise tasks. Not all tasks are created equal. Some will be critical to the progression of other tasks, while others can be shifted around without much impact.

Begin by identifying your critical path; these are the tasks that directly affect the completion date of your project. Any delay in these tasks will push everything back. For example, laying the foundation is a critical task in an extension project. Without it, nothing else can proceed.

Once you've highlighted these, assess which tasks can be parallelised. Perhaps while the electrician is wiring your new extension, the plumber can start fitting pipes in another part of the house. Maximising these opportunities can shave weeks off your project timeline.

Also, think about the impact of each task. Installing a new kitchen might be high on your priority list because it significantly affects your daily life. On the other hand, choosing curtain fittings, while important, may not need immediate attention.

Effective prioritisation not only accelerates the project but also helps in managing your budget more efficiently. By focusing on what's critical, you allocate resources where they are most needed, ensuring that your project moves forward without unnecessary expenditure on time or money.

## Contingency Planning

Even with the best-laid plans, the unexpected can happen. This is where contingency planning comes into play. It's about being prepared for the if's and but's that might throw a wrench in your works.

First, integrate buffer times into your schedule. These are small pockets of time set aside to absorb any project delays without affecting the overall timeline. Think of them as mini shock absorbers for your schedule. For instance, if you have a task that's supposed to take one week, consider scheduling ten days for it instead.

Next, prepare a contingency budget. Typically, setting aside an additional 10-20% of your total project cost can save you from heartache should prices rise unexpectedly or additional repairs be needed. It's much like taking an umbrella out when there's a forecast of rain — better safe than sorry.

Lastly, maintain open lines of communication with your team. Make sure everyone, from contractors to suppliers, knows that they can come to you with bad news as much as good. The sooner you know about a potential delay, the quicker you can act to mitigate it. Regular check-ins can help you stay ahead of any issues that might arise.

By mastering these elements of scheduling and timelines, you transform from a hopeful homeowner into a savvy project manager. Your home improvement project becomes less of a wild ride and more of a well-orchestrated symphony. With a realistic timeline, prioritised tasks, and robust contingency planning, you are set to steer your project toward timely and successful completion.

## Site Safety and Security

### Ensuring Worker Safety

When it comes to home improvements, the safety of everyone on-site should be your top priority. It's crucial to understand that a safe work environment not only protects workers but also ensures efficiency and keeps your project on track. To start, engage only with contractors who are committed to following health and safety regulations. This might mean spending a bit more time vetting your options, but the payoff in reliability and peace of mind is well worth it.

First things first, ensure that your contractor has a solid Health and Safety policy in place. This includes risk assessments for all tasks to be performed and method statements explaining how job risks are managed. Ask to see these documents. If they aren't provided upfront, consider it a red flag.

Next, make sure there's clear signage around the worksite. Signs should indicate areas that require protective gear, like hard hats or high-visibility jackets. It's also wise to check that there is accessible and well-maintained safety equipment, such as fire extinguishers and first aid kits. Regular safety briefings and meetings can keep safety protocols fresh in everyone's minds and encourage vigilance.

Remember, maintaining a tidy site can significantly reduce accidents. Insist that your team keeps their work areas clean and free from obstructions. Tools and materials should be securely stored at the end of each day to prevent any tripping hazards or other risks.

Lastly, consider the unique aspects of your project and any additional safety measures that might be needed. For example, if you're extending your home, ensure that the structural stability is maintained throughout the build to prevent collapses. If you're unsure about specific risks, consulting with a health and safety expert can be a valuable investment.

## Securing the Site

Securing your site is as much about preventing theft and vandalism as it is about safety. A secure site is a deterrent to those who might see your renovation as an opportunity for mischief or worse.

Start by ensuring that all entries and exits to the site are controlled. This might mean installing fences and gates with secure locks. It's also worth considering CCTV cameras as they are a great deterrent and can be crucial in the event of an incident. Make sure these security measures are visible; often, the mere presence of security equipment is enough to discourage potential intruders.

Lighting plays a crucial role in security too. Well-lit areas are less likely to attract unwanted visitors. Ensure that there are no dark corners or poorly lit areas where someone could hide or go unnoticed. Motion-activated lights can be particularly effective and energy-efficient.

During the project, you'll likely have a variety of tools and materials on site, which can be tempting targets for theft. To manage this, create a robust system for tracking equipment and materials. Consider having a secure storage solution, such as a lockable shed or storage container, where tools and materials can be kept when not in use. It's also wise to have a sign-in/sign-out system for tools, especially for those that are expensive or critical to your project.

## Neighbour Considerations

Last but definitely not least, let's talk about the neighbours. Managing your relationship with them during a build is crucial for maintaining both security and peace. Start by informing them of your plans well in advance. This gives them time to prepare for any disturbances and shows that you respect their peace and comfort.

During the build, ensure that your site is as unobtrusive as possible. This means controlling noise levels, managing dust, and keeping the site visually tidy. Regular updates can also go a long way; keeping your neighbours informed about the progress of the project and any potentially disruptive activities planned can help alleviate their concerns and maintain good relations.

Furthermore, secure boundaries such as fences not only keep your site safe but also prevent any materials or debris from spilling into your neighbour's property. Make sure that any shared access ways remain clear and accessible.

In the event of unexpected issues, such as damage to a neighbour's property, address these immediately. Taking responsibility and resolving issues swiftly can prevent a lot of bad blood and potentially expensive legal problems.

By keeping these three key areas in check — ensuring worker safety, securing the site, and considering the neighbours — you'll be on your way to managing a smooth and secure home improvement project. Remember, the goal is to enhance your home without compromising on the safety and security of those around you.

# Quality Control

When diving into the world of home improvements, maintaining a high standard of quality is not just a preference—it's a necessity. Ensuring that every phase of your project meets specific standards and compliances, from the initial materials used to the finishing touches, prevents future headaches and preserves the value of your property. Let's break down the essential components for maintaining quality control during your home renovation or extension project.

## Standards and Compliance

Navigating the maze of building regulations and standards can be daunting, but it's crucial for the legal and safe completion of your home improvements. Start by familiarising yourself with the Building Regulations applicable in your area. These regulations are designed to ensure that the work meets national standards for design, construction, and alterations. They cover everything from structural integrity and fire safety to energy efficiency and accessibility.

It's wise to engage with an architect or a surveyor who is well-versed in these matters. These professionals can provide invaluable guidance through the compliance jungle, helping you to understand which parts of your project may need special attention or certification. For instance, if you're planning to knock down walls for a more open plan living area, you'll need to consider the structural support and potentially involve a structural engineer.

Moreover, staying compliant isn't just about ticking off boxes to keep the council happy. It's about ensuring the safety and longevity of your home. For example, proper insulation standards can make or break the energy efficiency of your property, affecting utility bills and comfort for years to come.

## Regular Inspections

Think of regular inspections as your ongoing reality check during the construction process. These are not just formalities; they are your opportunities to catch issues before they become entrenched problems. Schedule inspections at various stages of the project, depending on the complexity and length of the job. Common stages include foundation laying, framing, roofing, electrical and plumbing, and final pre-plastering.

Hiring an independent inspector can provide an objective assessment that might overlook personal biases or oversight from your building team. These professionals will look at the work with a critical eye, comparing what they see against the plans and the regulatory requirements. It's their job to spot anything amiss before it's too late to rectify without major disruptions or costs.

Remember, effective communication with your builders is essential. Ensure they understand from the outset that regular inspections are part of the process and are not negotiable. This sets a professional tone and demonstrates your commitment to quality. After each inspection, discuss any issues with the construction team and make sure there is a clear plan and timeline for addressing them.

## Final Walkthroughs

The final walkthrough of your project is your last line of defence in quality control. This is your opportunity to ensure that everything has been completed to your satisfaction, in line with the agreed plans and to the quality you expect. Prepare for this stage by having a checklist based on the initial project scope and details. Include everything from the function of electrical sockets and fixtures to the finish on kitchen units and paintwork.

During the walkthrough, take your time and examine each element closely. Open and close doors and windows to check their fit and function, test taps, and look over surfaces for any unfinished areas or defects. Don't rush this process. If you spot problems, list them and discuss how they can be rectified with your contractor.

If possible, have the final inspection done in the presence of the contractor. This helps to immediately address any concerns and facilitates a direct conversation about any corrective actions needed. It's not uncommon for minor tweaks to be required, so negotiate a clear timeline for these final adjustments.

Remember, the goal of the final walkthrough is not just to critique but to confirm that the project you've envisioned and invested in has been realised to the standards you set out. This step is crucial not only for your satisfaction but also for the overall success of the renovation or extension.

In the realm of home improvements, the adage "trust, but verify" could not be more pertinent. By actively engaging in each step of the quality control process, from understanding the standards and compliance required, through regular inspections, to thorough final walkthroughs, you can ensure that your project not only meets but exceeds expectations. This approach not only safeguards your investment but also ensures that the finished product is something you can be proud of for years to come.

## RECAP AND ACTION ITEMS

Congratulations on making it through the "Managing the Build" chapter. You're now equipped with the strategic insights needed to oversee your home improvement project effectively. Let's ensure you can put this knowledge into action.

Firstly, take some time to draft a detailed plan that incorporates everything you've learned about Scheduling and Timelines. Create a realistic timeline for your project, prioritising tasks to maintain momentum and including a contingency plan to handle any unforeseen circumstances. Use tools like Gantt charts or project management software to keep things organised and transparent. Remember, a well-planned schedule is your roadmap to timely and stress-free completion.

Next, focus on Site Safety and Security. Ensuring the safety of everyone on-site is paramount. Conduct regular safety audits and make sure all workers are familiar with safety protocols. Secure your site at the end of each day to protect materials and equipment from theft or damage. Don't forget to maintain good relations with your neighbours by keeping them informed about your plans, especially about any aspects that might affect them such as noise or boundary adjustments.

Moving on to Quality Control, establish clear standards and compliance from the start. Regular inspections are crucial; consider hiring an independent inspector to review the work at critical stages. Plan for a thorough final walkthrough to catch any issues before signing off on the project. This step is crucial to ensure the longevity and safety of your improvements.

Now, take these structured steps and apply them diligently to your project. Keep this guide handy and refer back to it at each phase of your project. Good management is not just about following steps; it's about adapting to situations with a clear head and a strategic approach. Your home improvement journey just got a whole lot smoother. Happy building!

# 10

# ENJOYING YOUR TRANSFORMED HOME

*"a house is made with walls and beams; a home is built with love and dreams."*
  *~ Ralph Waldo Emerson*

## Post-Construction Care

Congratulations, your home transformation project is complete! But, hang on a minute, the journey doesn't end here. Now that the dust has settled, literally and metaphorically, it's crucial to shift your focus towards keeping your newly renovated space in top condition. Let's dive into the essential elements of post-construction care: maintenance tips, warranties and guarantees, and long-term care strategies.

## Maintenance Tips

Firstly, maintaining your home post-renovation is key to ensuring your space remains as impressive as the day the contractors packed up. Regular upkeep not only keeps your home looking great but also helps in avoiding costly repairs down the line.

Start with a thorough post-construction clean-up. This isn't just about aesthetics; leftover construction materials can be hazardous. Hire professional cleaners who specialise in post-construction cleaning to ensure all debris, dust, and potentially harmful materials are completely removed. This can be particularly important in avoiding issues like poor indoor air quality, which can impact your health.

Next, establish a routine inspection schedule. Check areas like roofing, plumbing, and electrical systems every few months. Look out for any small issues that could turn into major problems if left unattended. For instance, a small leak under a newly installed sink can lead to significant water damage over time if not addressed.

For areas that endure high usage, such as kitchen counters or bathroom fittings, regular checks are vital. Materials can degrade, and mechanisms can wear out. Knowing the typical lifespan of these materials and fixtures helps you anticipate replacements before they fail unexpectedly.

Additionally, consider the external elements of your home. For instance, if you've added an extension with a new roof, regularly clearing gutters and inspecting roof tiles after heavy weather can prevent water ingress and structural damage.

## Warranty and Guarantees

When your renovation project wraps up, make sure you have all your warranty documents organised and accessible. Most new appliances and systems come with manufacturer warranties. Understanding these guarantees can save you a lot of hassle and money. For instance, if your new eco-friendly boiler stops functioning correctly, knowing the warranty terms can facilitate a quick resolution, often at no extra cost.

But warranties aren't just about appliances. If your renovation involved structural work, like underpinning or new construction, these areas might also be covered by warranties from your building contractor. It's essential to have a clear understanding of what is covered under these warranties. Typically, they cover defects in materials and workmanship. Be sure to clarify how long the warranty lasts and any specific maintenance obligations required to keep it valid.

Keep a file with all warranty documents and service records. If a problem arises, this organised approach will help you to quickly verify whether it's covered by a warranty and liaise effectively with the service providers.

## Long-Term Care Strategies

Thinking long-term is crucial when it comes to your renovated home. Long-term care involves planning for eventualities and ensuring your home adapts to changing needs and technologies.

One aspect of long-term care is budgeting for future repairs and updates. Setting aside a portion of your household budget for home maintenance ensures you are prepared for any unexpected issues. Also, consider creating a timeline for possible upgrades in the future, such as replacing older appliances with more energy-efficient models as they reach the end of their useful life.

Another strategy involves staying updated with technological advancements. The world of home automation and energy efficiency is constantly evolving. Systems that manage heating, lighting, and security remotely can not only provide convenience but also offer significant cost savings in the long run. Keeping an eye on these developments can help you incorporate new technologies into your home, keeping it modern and efficient.

Moreover, adapting your home for future life stages can be a wise strategy. For example, if you plan to stay in your home into old age, consider incorporating age-friendly features such as wider doorways, one-level layouts, or walk-in showers during your initial renovation. This foresight can save you from undertaking another major renovation later in life.

In conclusion, post-construction care is about more than just dealing with the immediate aftermath of a renovation. It's about taking proactive steps to maintain, protect, and future-proof your investment. By following these tips on maintenance, understanding and utilising warranties, and planning for the long-term, you ensure that your home remains safe, functional, and beautiful for many years to come.

## Evaluating the Impact on Property Value

When you've put in the sweat, time, and possibly a significant part of your savings into upgrading your home, it's only natural to wonder about the kind of return you might see if you decide to sell. Property value isn't just about what you feel your home is worth; it's also about hard numbers that reflect its market value. Let's dive into how your home improvements could translate into real financial gains.

### Appraisal Considerations

First off, getting your home appraised after significant improvements is a smart move. An appraisal gives you a professional evaluation of your home's market value, and post-renovation, it's likely to have shifted. The key here is understanding what appraisers look for and how they determine the value added by your upgrades.

Appraisers will look at your home's size, condition, location, and the quality and value of any improvements. Structural changes like room additions or major kitchen remodels often bring the highest returns in terms of appraisal value. However, smaller updates like new windows or an upgraded heating system can also positively impact the appraisal value by increasing your home's energy efficiency.

Make sure your improvements are well-documented. Keep receipts, contracts, and before-and-after photos. These can provide an appraiser with clear evidence of the enhancements made, making it easier for them to assess the true value added to your property.

Remember, though, that not all renovations offer the same bang for your buck. Luxury upgrades in a modest neighbourhood might not yield high returns due to what appraisers call "over-improvement." Your home's value can't exceed the typical market value of other homes in your area by too much, even if it has superior features.

## Market Trends

Understanding the current market trends is crucial when evaluating how your property improvements will impact your home's value. Property markets can fluctuate based on economic conditions, changes in supply and demand, and other external factors like interest rates or government policies.

For instance, if there's a trend towards working from home, adding an office space might have more value now than it would have a few years ago. Similarly, in areas where sustainability is valued, investments in eco-friendly technologies can significantly increase a property's appeal and value.

Stay informed about the local real estate market by following reports from estate agents, attending community meetings, and reading up on property market analyses. This knowledge will not only help you understand the potential increase in your property value but will also equip you with the insights needed to plan any future improvements in line with market demands.

## Return on Investment

Lastly, let's talk about the return on investment (ROI), which is essentially what you get back from what you've put in. Not all home improvements offer a high ROI, so choosing the right projects is key to enhancing your property value. Generally, projects that improve the overall functionality and appeal of the home tend to offer better returns.

For example, kitchen renovations and adding or updating bathrooms are known for their potential to increase home value. According to several studies, you might expect to recover anywhere from50% to85% of your investment on a major kitchen remodel when you sell your home, depending on the scale and the specifics of the renovation.

Another aspect to consider is the quality of the finishes used. High-quality, durable materials can attract more buyers and possibly increase the offer price. However, there is a balance to be struck, as overly personalised choices might not appeal to the general market.

Improvements that enhance your home's energy efficiency can also lead to substantial ROI not only through market value but through savings on utility costs. Features like solar panels, upgraded insulation, or high-efficiency windows can be appealing selling points that are increasingly attractive to today's environmentally conscious buyers.

While it's tempting to follow current trends, consider the longevity of such improvements. Classic, timeless updates might appeal to a broader audience when the time comes to sell.

In conclusion, understanding these elements — appraisal considerations, market trends, and potential ROI — will give you a clearer picture of how your home improvements have changed not just your living environment but also your financial landscape. Armed with this knowledge, you can make informed decisions about future projects and possibly maximise the financial benefits when it's time to sell.

## Living and Thriving in Your New Space

## Adapting to New Layouts

So, you've knocked down walls, thrown up some new ones, and maybe even added a skylight or two. Your home's layout has transformed, and now it's time to make the best of this new world. Adapting isn't just about figuring out where the sofa looks best (though that's important too); it's about creating a flow that complements your daily routines and enhances your lifestyle.

Begin by considering the journey you take from room to room. Does the new layout encourage a natural flow of movement? Are there areas where traffic might bottleneck, especially during busy mornings or when entertaining guests? Sometimes what looks good on paper doesn't translate perfectly into real life, and you might need small adjustments to perfect your space.

Think about each room's function and the placement of furniture and features. For instance, in your newly positioned kitchen, ensure that the 'work triangle' between the sink, fridge, and cooker is compact to aid in efficient meal prep. In the living area, consider the layout's sociability aspect—does it foster conversation, or does the new arrangement feel a bit too spread out?

Moreover, if your renovation included adding new, smart technology, take the time to familiarise yourself with its features. Smart thermostats, lighting systems, and security features can significantly enhance your living experience, but only if used correctly. Spend an afternoon playing around with the settings to find what works best for your lifestyle.

Lastly, give yourself time to get used to the changes. Just like a new pair of shoes, a new layout needs a bit of breaking in. You'll soon find the rhythm and quirks of your new space, turning it from a house to a home.

## Energy Efficiency Benefits

Upgrading your home isn't just about aesthetics and comfort; it's also a chance to dial up the efficiency and dial down the costs. If your renovations included energy-efficient improvements, you're likely to notice the differences not just in your comfort levels, but also in your energy bills.

Start with insulation—walls, roofs, and floors. Good insulation keeps your home warmer in the winter and cooler in the summer, reducing the need for constant heating or air conditioning. If you've included high-quality insulation in your renovation, you should start seeing reduced thermal fluctuations and a more consistent indoor environment.

Windows play a huge role too. Double or triple-glazed windows can significantly reduce heat loss. They're an investment that pays dividends not just in energy savings but also in reducing outside noise, which is a boon if you're near a busy street.

Then there's the heart of your home's energy consumption: heating and cooling systems. Modern, energy-efficient systems can be tailored much more closely to your needs with programmable thermostats and even zone-specific controls, allowing you to heat or cool only the areas you're using. Plus, with the advent of smart home technologies, you can manage these systems remotely, ensuring you're only using energy when and where it's needed.

Renewable energy sources, such as solar panels, might also be part of your renovation. These can reduce your dependence on external energy sources and might even earn you some money back if you generate more power than you use. Check how your system is performing and look into feed-in tariffs to see if you can get credit for your excess energy.

## Personal Satisfaction and Comfort

Now, let's talk about the heart of the matter: how these changes make you feel. After all, the primary goal of home improvement is to improve the quality of life for you and your family. With your new and improved home, you should find that your environment aligns more closely with your personal needs and aesthetic preferences, which can significantly boost your overall happiness and comfort.

Reflect on the choices you made during the renovation process— perhaps you chose a particular paint colour because it made you feel peaceful, or opted for an open-plan layout to gather more as a family. These decisions are not just functional; they're deeply personal and contribute to a sense of well-being.

Comfort isn't just physical; it's also psychological. A home that reflects your personal style can serve as a sanctuary from the outside world, a place where you can truly relax and be yourself. Whether it's through the inclusion of cosy nooks perfect for reading, expansive windows that bring the outdoors in, or an entertainment room that brings your family together, each element contributes to making your home a haven.

Finally, there's the satisfaction of accomplishment. Completing a home renovation project, especially one that drastically transforms your space, is no small feat. It's a tangible result of your planning, decision-making, and investment—an achievement that not only adds value to your property but also enhances your everyday life.

Each day, as you live in and move through your transformed home, you'll experience the myriad benefits of your efforts: improved functionality, increased comfort, and a deep sense of personal satisfaction. These are the true rewards of home improvement, making all the challenges and decisions along the way worth it. Enjoy your new space to the fullest—you've earned it!

## RECAP AND ACTION ITEMS

Congratulations on navigating the journey of transforming your home! By now, you should have a solid grasp of maintaining your upgraded space, understanding its increased value, and relishing the new lifestyle it affords. Here's a quick roundup of actionable steps to ensure you continue to benefit from your home improvements effectively and enjoyably.

Firstly, keep the pulse on the maintenance of your home. Regularly schedule checks and adhere to the maintenance tips provided. This proactive approach will prevent minor issues from ballooning into costly repairs. Organise your documents related to warranties and guarantees in an accessible manner, ensuring you can leverage them swiftly if something goes awry.

Next, stay informed about your property's value. Even if you're not looking to sell soon, understanding the appraisal considerations and staying updated on market trends will equip you with the knowledge to make informed decisions about further investments or adjustments in your property. Periodically review the return on investment for your renovations, refining your strategy to enhance your property's value continually.

Lastly, fully immerse yourself in the joy and functionality of your new living space. Adapt to the new layouts by experimenting with different setups that might enhance your daily routine. Embrace the energy efficiency benefits not only as a cost-saving measure but as a contribution to a greener planet. Most importantly, ensure that your renovated home continues to meet your needs for personal satisfaction and comfort. Make adjustments where necessary, and remember, your home should be your sanctuary.

In summary, your transformed home is not just a static asset but a dynamic space that evolves with your life's changes and challenges. Keep it maintained, understand its value, and most importantly, enjoy it to the fullest. Take these steps, and you'll not only secure your investment but also enhance your quality of life. Here's to a home that continues to inspire and comfort you, every single day!

# EMBARK ON YOUR TRANSFORMATION JOURNEY

As you turn the pages of this guide, you've journeyed through a comprehensive exploration of unlocking the hidden potential within your home. Each chapter has not only aimed to inspire but also to empower you with the knowledge and innovative strategies necessary to transform ordinary spaces into extraordinary living areas. The essence of this exploration goes beyond mere renovation; it's about reimagining your living environment to enhance your quality of life.

Imagine stepping into your home where every corner is optimised, every space is utilised to its fullest potential. This isn't just about adding value to your property; it's about creating environments that uplift your spirits, spaces that reflect your personality, and settings that function at their peak. You have the blueprint; now, it's time to act.

Envision your home after you've applied the insights from the chapters on loft conversions, extensions, and garage transformations. Picture the increased functionality and aesthetic appeal. Think about the satisfaction of utilising every square metre to its maximum potential. This vision is within your reach and now, more than ever, it's crucial to take those first steps towards making it a reality.

The process of transforming your home is a significant journey, and while the road may seem daunting, the reward at the end is immeasurably fulfilling. It's about crafting a space that not only meets your needs but also exceeds your expectations. It's about not just meeting the standard but setting new benchmarks in personalised living.

However, knowing where to start or how to navigate the complexities of planning and executing such transformations can be challenging. Questions like "What permissions do I need?" or "How do I ensure the quality of the work?" are likely on your mind. This is why seeking professional guidance is not just beneficial but essential.

Professionals in home transformation can offer you not only their expertise in design and construction but also their experience in managing such projects from concept to completion. They understand the nuances of maximising space while adhering to regulatory standards and can help you avoid common pitfalls that might cost you time and money.

If you feel inspired to take your home to the next level after reading this guide, I encourage you not to let this moment pass. Reach out for professional help to discuss your ideas and start laying down the plans for your project. Whether it's refining the concepts you've read about here or tailoring unique solutions for your space, the right professional can turn your vision into reality.

Remember, every great journey begins with a single step. Take that step today and begin the exciting process of transforming your home into a place that not only looks spectacular but feels uniquely yours. It's time to realise the potential of your home, to create spaces that not only serve functional purposes but also provide comfort and joy to those who inhabit them.

In conclusion, let this guide serve as your inspiration and your call to action. The concepts and ideas presented here are just the beginning. With professional guidance, your journey towards a transformed home can be smooth, efficient, and incredibly rewarding. Reach out today, and start turning your dream home into a reality. Your future self will thank you for making such a life-enhancing decision.

Transform your space, transform your life.

Printed in Great Britain
by Amazon